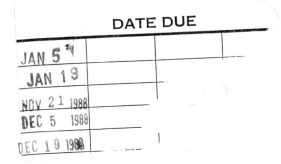

Master of Ballyhoo
The Story of P. T. Barnum

ONE of his most famous remarks—and it was probably twisted—was "There's a sucker born every minute." But, in truth, he seldom made a sucker out of anyone, and in the long run he gave more people more entertainment for their money than his ten nearest competitors. His methods for setting up his many museums and exhibits were sometimes devious, but he was nevertheless the greatest showman who ever lived. Five generations will remember him for such extravaganzas as the bright midget, General Tom Thumb, the Cardiff Giant hoax, the lyrical and triumphant tour of Jenny Lind, and finally the mammoth circus of all times, still known as the Greatest Show on Earth.

PHINEAS TAYLOR BARNUM
Photo, courtesy of Elizabeth Sterling Seeley,
Historian, The Barnum Museum, Bridgeport, Connecticut

Master of Ballyhoo

The Story of
P. T. Barnum

By Felix Sutton

FOUNDED 1838

GPPS

G. P. PUTNAM'S SONS, NEW YORK

*For Geoffrey Coe Sutton,
who is tolerably versed
in the art of ballyhoo*

Contents

Master of Ballyhoo
The Story of
P. T. Barnum

1

The Laziest Boy in Town

JULY THE FOURTH, 1810, was a glorious day in Bethel, Connecticut. Boys set off firecrackers and torpedoes in the dusty dirt road that served as the town's main street—spooking the farmers' horses.

The local unit of the Connecticut militia marched raggedly down the street shouldering flintlock muskets. They were preceded by a handful of grizzled veterans of the Revolutionary War who carried the flag of the infant United States—which in that day consisted of fifteen stars and fifteen stripes. The Bethel schoolmaster, Professor Zerah Judson, delivered a patriotic oration from the steps of Mr. Stiles Wakelee's tavern. A young man from the nearby Danbury Academy read the Declaration of Independence with dramatic gestures.

The ceremonies finally done with, the militiamen and

veterans retired to Mr. Wakelee's bar to toast the great day in mugs of ale or cherry rum.

But the Fourth of July was just about the only occasion when the good folks of Bethel, or nearly any other New England community for that matter, were allowed to do anything as frivolous as have a little organized fun. For the rest of the year, throughout practically all of the northeastern United States, it was considered almost sinful for Americans to act as though they were enjoying themselves.

No one knows exactly why the laws against pleasure in New England were called "blue laws"—although the term may have come down from the age-old custom of English churches being decorated in blue colors on the Monday before Lent. In any case, Connecticut laws were "blue" indeed, and they were strictly enforced by the deacons of the church. If a man rode his horse on Sunday, or failed to go to church services, or criticized the preacher's sermon, or muttered a cussword when something went wrong, or played cards, or even slept late—if he committed any of these dreadful sins, he could be arrested by a deacon and thrown into jail or be publicly horsewhipped on the village green.

Even in big cities such as New York, life was dreary. Parties were rare. The few theaters were attended only by those hardy dissenters who didn't believe that watching a play would doom them to the eternal fires. About the only sources of amusement were the museums that exhibited moth-eaten curiosities in the name of education.

But on that July 4, 1810, in a little upstairs bedroom in a story-and-a-half house in Bethel, Mrs. Philo Barnum, the wife of a part-time farmer and part-time storekeeper, was awaiting the birth of her first baby—a boy who was destined to knock down most of the blue-law bugaboos, and who would make fun and good times a respectable part of the American way of life.

He came into the world a day later, on July 5.

"I'd have enjoyed being born on the Fourth of July," P. T. Barnum once said after he had become famous as the world's greatest showman. "But maybe my tardiness was for the best. Competition between Barnum and Independence Day would have been too much. As it was, I made my appearance after peace and quiet had been restored and the audience had regained its seats."

He was named Phineas Taylor, after his maternal grandfather, and it was probably from that nonconforming old gentleman that young P. T. inherited his love of the ludicrous and the bizarre. Old Phineas Taylor was the town wag. He would go to any length to pull off a practical joke. As a matter of fact, he began playing one on his infant grandson the very day the child was born. It was a gigantic joke that kept on growing and building up for more than ten years—and one that everybody in Bethel, except young P. T. Barnum, of course, was in on. But, it later provided the slender thread of security that got Barnum started in show business.

As a christening gift, Grandpa Taylor gave his namesake a deed to five acres of land situated in a remote part of Bethel parish and known as Ivy Island. It was a barren rise in the middle of a dismal swamp, bearing only stunted trees and huge growths of briars and poison ivy, and thickly inhabited by wasps, hornets, lizards and snakes. But his grandfather always referred to P. T. as the "richest lad in the state," since he owned such a valuable piece of farmland. His mother and father took great delight in going along with the gag.

"Taylor," his father would say seriously, "I hope that when you grow up and inherit your property you won't forget to do something for your mother and me."

Barnum was ten years old before he saw Ivy Island. Then, on a summer day, his father informed him that they were going to take in some hay from the meadow that adjoined it, and that he might at last visit his estate.

Bright and early the next morning the haying party set out. When they arrived at the meadow, P. T. asked his father where Ivy Island was located.

"Yonder, my boy," his father replied, "where you see those beautiful trees rising in the distance."

All morning Barnum worked like fury, turning the grass with a pitchfork as fast as his father and a jovial Irish farmhand named Edmund could scythe it. Then, at noon, Edmund put down his scythe, shouldered an ax, and announced that he was ready to take the boy to see his property.

A swamp began at the end of the meadow, and the pair soon found themselves leaping from one clump of sawgrass to another to keep out of the watery muck. After about half a mile, they came to a little stream, its banks covered by thick stands of alders and briers.

"Now, lad," the hired man said, grinning, "we have only to cross this creek, and we will be on your own valuable property." He then felled a small tree with his axe to serve as an "Indian bridge."

Wide-eyed, the boy rushed across it and, at long last, stood on Ivy Island.

"When I looked around me at the barren, worthless piece of wilderness," Barnum wrote later, "the truth came upon me in a flash. I had been the laughingstock of my family and neighbors for years." As he stood there, contemplating his sudden downfall, a large black snake approached him with head upraised and red tongue flicking. With a shriek, the boy ran for the makeshift bridge and the safety of the hayfield. This was his first, and last, visit to Ivy Island.

Young Taylor Barnum's formal education was, at best, touch-and-go. He started attending the Bethel district school at the age of six, and was one of the "brightest boys" in his class. But after two or three years, he was out of school more than he was in. Like all farm boys of that time and place, he had to split firewood, plant corn, chop weeds and, as he grew older, help with the plowing. When he was about twelve, his father bought a small store in Bethel and Taylor was installed as chief clerk. One summer term at the Danbury Academy marked the end of P. T.'s short-lived tussle with education.

But Barnum was happier clerking in a store than going to school or hoeing corn. Head-work had always been a great deal more to his liking than hand-work, and all his young life he had gone to great lengths to avoid physical labor. "I believe," he once said, "that I had the reputation of being the laziest boy in town."

Yet, Barnum was never lazy from the neck up. And the lessons he learned behind the counter of his father's store had a far greater effect upon his future than those he learned bending over a desk at the Academy. They honed his wits to a fine edge and sharpened his instincts for driving a hard bargain—talents that were to make millions for him when he became the world's first great showman.

His father's store, as did all country stores in those days, accepted such commodities as eggs, butter, rags and grain in exchange for axes, knives, scythes, salt, sugar, clothing and other items that the customers needed. Many was the time a farm woman came in with a bundle of rags which she declared to be all linen or cotton, only to have Taylor open them for inspection and find worthless trash and even stones and pebbles hidden away inside.

Or a farmer might bring in a wagonload of fifty bushels of oats, which Barnum would find, upon weighing it, was four or five bushels short. Then the farmer would get red with rage and howl: "Dang that no-good farm hand of mine! He never *could* count nohow!"

P. T. Barnum always liked the feel of money. When he was only ten, he began doing a thriving business with the members of the militia when the citizen-soldiers came to town to drill on the village green. His two chief stocks-in-trade were "cookania," a sort of taffy boiled down from molasses, and cherry rum, which he made by flavoring raw New England rum with crushed wild cherries and a little sugar. As soon as he heard the captain's order: "At ease!" he rushed over to the worn-out militiamen with his demijohn and tin cup, and always did a sell-out business. With the proceeds, he bought a sheep and a calf, as well as all his own clothing. He was a capitalist before he was twelve.

Looking around for other ways to add to the growing pile of pennies, dimes and dollars that he kept in a jam pot under the eaves of the attic, Taylor soon latched onto the idea of managing a lottery. In those days, lotteries were legal—and often ministers promoted them for the benefit of their churches, even though they stood up in the pulpit on Sundays and preached against the evils of gambling.

Grandpa Phineas Taylor had run private lotteries for years, and he advised his ambitious grandson: "Get into the lottery business, Taylor, and you'll be rich overnight."

The price of chances was small and so were the prizes.

There was always enough clear profit to go into the bulging jam pot. Then suddenly, overnight, the little world of the Barnums came tumbling down.

In 1825, when Taylor was fifteen, his father died—and when the estate was settled he was bankrupt. Taylor had loaned his jam-pot savings to his father in a last-ditch effort to keep the family business going. But the court ruled that since he was a minor he had no claim on any part of the estate's meager assets. And so, at the age of fifteen, P. T. Barnum was also bankrupt—and being the oldest child, he had a family to support as well.

For a time he clerked in a store in Grassy Plains, a village about a mile from Bethel. And even though he chafed at the idea of working for someone else, he was such a go-getting clerk and shrewd trader that his employers, James Keeler and Lewis Witlock, gave him every chance they could to promote private ventures for himself.

One day an itinerant peddler stopped at the store with a wagon full of ordinary green glass bottles. Since both his employers were out of town, Barnum took it upon himself to make a deal. He bought the whole load of bottles in exchange for a pile of unsalable junk that had been cluttering up the back of the store for years. The peddler, taking Taylor for a green kid, figured that he had gotten the best of the bargain and happily went on his way.

When Mr. Keeler got back to his store that evening, he was flabbergasted to find it half filled with worthless bottles.

"Taylor, you've made a fool of yourself," he said, shaking his head. "You've got enough bottles here to supply the whole town for twenty years."

But Barnum had not bought the bottles just for the fun of making a deal. Also in a corner of the back storeroom was a large collection of ancient tinware—nutmeg graters, milk skimmers, tin cups, flour scoops and the like—that had been collecting rust and flyspecks since probably before Barnum was born. When he had made the bottle trade he had a scheme in the back of his head that would get rid of the entire lot of surplus merchandise in one grand clearance sale.

Without revealing his plan, he assured his employer that the bottles would be gone in no time.

Mr. Keeler was skeptical. "If you can do that," he said, "you can perform a miracle."

So young P. T. Barnum made a miracle to order. He hand-lettered a poster which he tacked up on the front of the Keeler & Whitlock store. It read:

MAGNIFICENT LOTTERY!
$25 FOR ONLY 50 CENTS!
OVER 550 PRIZES!
ONLY 1,000 TICKETS!

Almost everybody in Grassy Plains, as well as in Bethel, Redding and Georgetown, bought chances. They were sold out in a week. Then the drawing took place, and the lucky winners lined up for their prizes.

The grand prize was $25, payable in any kind of goods the customer desired. As for the rest of the prizes, they consisted mostly of green glass bottles and ancient tinware. A housewife, say, who had won five dollars' worth of merchandise might get a spool of cotton thread, a paper of pins, fifteen or sixteen cream skimmers and nutmeg graters and a few dozen bottles of assorted sizes. Another winner would get nothing but glass bottles or a collection of tin cups and flour scoops. Within a week or ten days, all the bottles and old tinware were gone.

Some of the winners protested, but for the most part,

being New Englanders, they took their fleecing with a wry grin.

Grandpa Taylor was beside himself with glee. "Sonny boy," he said, wiping tears of laughter out of his eyes, "you're a chip off the old block, and that's for certain."

Keeler and Whitlock sold their Grassy Plains store in 1827—and this gave Taylor Barnum a chance to move on. A distant relative, Oliver Taylor, had moved from Danbury to open a general store in Brooklyn, New York, a few years before, and now he offered Barnum a job as clerk. Many of the residents of Brooklyn arose early in the morning to buy food for breakfast before going to work. Although a country boy, young P. T. had always been something of a late sleeper and he couldn't get used to the idea of getting up before daylight. So he worked out a deal with the night watchman of the building. Each night when he went to bed he tied a string around his big toe and let the other end hang out the window of his upstairs sleeping quarters. Whenever a particularly early-bird customer showed up, the watchman would yank on the string and P. T. would hustle down to the store in his nightshirt. The arrangement worked—even though, in the process, it gave young Mr. Barnum a chronically sore big toe.

It took just about a year for Taylor Barnum to decide that he wasn't cut out for working for wages, especially in 1827, when a clerk's wages were exceedingly poor. The only bright hours of his life were those spent at the theater —such as it was in the New York of those days. He fell in love with show business—although he hadn't the faintest idea at the time that one day he would be the biggest showman who ever lived.

In February, 1828, he received a letter from his grandfather Taylor. The old man wrote that if Barnum returned to Bethel, he would give him, rent-free, one half of the ground floor of a building that he owned on the town's main street. P. T. decided at once that he would turn the place into a fruit and confectionery store.

He packed his few clothes into a battered carpetbag and was on his way back to the village of his birth.

2

Boy Businessman—Crusading Editor

EARLY on the first Monday morning in May, 1828, Taylor Barnum stood on the front porch of his new store and surveyed the sun-brightened world that he planned some day, somehow, to conquer.

Although not quite eighteen, he had the bearing of a grown man. He was six-feet-two and broad shouldered, with a big head that was covered by a mop of curly hair. His nose tended to be bulbous, and his face was deeply pockmarked by a severe attack of smallpox which he had suffered a year before.

He was also flat broke. He had come to Bethel with a total capital of $120, of which $50 had gone into remodeling the building, and the other $70 into buying his initial stock, which included a barrel of ale.

With true Yankee sagacity, he scheduled his grand opening for Militia Training Day. When he closed up shop that evening he discovered that he had made back almost his entire investment in retail sales. With this money, he went back to New York and laid in a supply of "fancy goods"—combs, beads, pocketbooks, knives and cheap toys.

Business was brisk all summer, and in the fall, upon his grandfather's advice, he took on the agency of a lottery dealer for a commission of 10 percent. But being a middleman wasn't P. T. Barnum's style. He went directly to the lottery managers in Hartford and convinced them he could handle a dealership. He then established branch offices in Danbury, Norwalk, Middletown and Stamford, as well as dozens of small agencies for some thirty miles around. After the business got under way, Taylor found that he was selling from 500 to 2,000 tickets a day. And "my profits," he wrote, "were immense."

It was about this time that Barnum's flair for advertising first showed up in a big way. Newspapers in the surrounding countryside bristled with the kind of advertisements people had never seen before: big, glaring capital letters, exclamation points, wood-block illustrations of fictitious winners who had won fabulous sums in the Barnum lotteries. He put out handbills of the same kind. The Yankees of southern Connecticut went "lottery crazy."

There was one minister in Brookfield who was a good friend of Grandpa Taylor, and with whom P. T. always ate supper when he happened to be in that town. Unfailingly, the minister would take young Barnum off to one side and purchase a few tickets, always exacting a solemn promise that his wife would never be told of the transaction. And when the preacher stepped out of the house to feed his horse or do some other chore, his wife would buy some tickets for herself, pledging Barnum to strict secrecy as far as her husband was concerned. A good salesman interested in future business, P. T. never told on either of them.

Ever since he had been sixteen and a clerk in the Keeler-Whitlock store, Taylor had been in love with a girl he had met in Grassy Plains. Their meeting was in the classic romantic tradition. The girl, Charity Hallett, had been in Grassy Plains for a Saturday afternoon. But in the late summer evening a furious thunderstorm came up. Charity was afraid to ride the mile to Bethel by herself. So the lady she had been visiting, a Mrs. Wheeler, knowing that Taylor Barnum always went home on Saturdays to spend Sunday with his family, asked him to see Charity safely to Bethel.

Upon arriving at Mrs. Wheeler's house, Barnum was introduced to Charity, whom he later described as "the most wondrous woman I have ever seen."

As they rode along the rain-drenched road, young P. T. fell in love. "At once," he later wrote, "I wished that the ride was five miles instead of one. And when a flash of lightning gave me a fair view of her face, I then wished that the ride could be twenty miles instead of five."

He saw Charity at church the next morning and was not able to take his eyes off her. But he only nodded to her after the service was over, and she, in turn, smiled.

The two had a few dates—although such meetings were not referred to as "dates" then—at church sociables and community affairs.

After his sojourn in Brooklyn, when he came back to Bethel to open his own store, he decided that the time had come to do something about Charity. After his store and his lottery business became a success, he timidly—and "timid" was rarely a word that was applied to P. T. Barnum—proposed. He was accepted, and arrangements were made for a fall marriage.

Charity was two years older than Taylor—he nineteen, she twenty-one. Taylor's mother thought that the girl was too old for him, and that, in any case, he should look for a more advantageous marriage. The Halletts, on the other hand, declared that their Charity was "altogether too good for the likes of Taylor Barnum."

In October they went separately to New York City—he on the pretext of buying supplies for the store, and she with the excuse that she wanted to visit a favorite uncle. There, in her uncle's house on Orchard Street, they were married.

Back in Bethel they lived in a boardinghouse until a modest home could be built for them on three acres that he had purchased from his grandfather—surely the most influential individual in P. T. Barnum's life.

The three years that followed were busy and exciting for the young businessman. He put up a building in Bethel and opened another store in partnership with his uncle, Alanson Taylor. He also started a book business, buying large quantities of books in New York and auctioning them off in little backwater Connecticut towns. But so many were stolen behind his back while he was making his auction pitches that he gave up book selling as a losing proposition.

When P. T. turned twenty-one and was eligible to vote, he became intensely interested in politics. A Jeffersonian Democrat, like his father and grandfather before him, he was outraged when a new party sprang up in Connecticut. Called a Church and State Party, it advocated that the old established church, with its Puritan concepts, be given a strong hand in the affairs of government.

To Barnum, this was in clear defiance of the Bill of Rights, and he began firing off letters of protest to the

Danbury *Recorder,* the only newspaper in the immediate vicinity. When the *Recorder*'s editor refused to print them, **P. T.**, with his usual zeal, decided to publish a paper of his own. Accordingly, he bought a printing press, and the first issue of *The Herald of Freedom,* P T. Barnum editor-in-chief and sole staff member, appeared on October 19, 1831.

His editorials attracted wide attention—and soon *The Herald of Freedom* had a limited circulation in every state in the Union, at a subscription price of $1.50 a year.

Considering his barefisted attacks, Barnum inevitably laid himself open to charges of libel. The first libel suit cost him what he later described as "several hundred dollars." In the second suit, he was found "not guilty." But the third one not only resulted in a $100 fine but also landed him in the Danbury jailhouse for sixty days.

This suit had been brought by a Bethel deacon whom Barnum had accused of *usury.* If the crusading young editor had used a word such as *extortion* or *note-shaving,* he would have been cleared—since his charge was substantially proved by a number of witnesses, and even admitted by the prosecuting deacon. But *usury* was specifically condemned in the Bible. And in church-dominated Connecticut, the Bible was the highest of all laws, from which there was no appeal.

Barnum's many friends—as well as newspaper editors from as far away as New Haven and Hartford—came to his support. His cell was brightly wallpapered and the floor was carpeted. Special food was brought to him—and scores of visitors flocked to the jail to congratulate him on what they referred to as his "martyrdom."

He continued to edit *The Herald of Freedom* from his

cell, and because of all the publicity created by his case the subscription list began to grow.

When the sixty-day sentence was up, a huge banquet was held in his honor in the very courtroom in which he had been tried. After the speeches, a triumphant parade was formed to escort Barnum to his home in Bethel, three miles away. It was headed by a Grand Marshall carrying The Stars and Stripes and leading a semimilitary escort of forty horsemen. Behind them came an extra-large six-horse coach that bore the guest of honor and a brass band that endlessly blared forth "Yankee Doodle," a new tune called "The Star-Spangled Banner" and other patriotic airs. Following Barnum's coach were sixty carriages filled with prominent citizens from all the towns around. The roads were lined on both sides by hundreds of cheering neighbors.

In reporting the gala affair in his paper, Barnum wrote: "We are happy to add that no accidents occurred to mar the festivities of the occasion."

This was P. T. Barnum's first real brush with fame—and from that day forth he could never be entirely happy unless he was in center stage.

But in his zealous concentration on his newspaper, Barnum had allowed his other business affairs to slide. The Connecticut Assembly had outlawed lotteries and he was caught overnight with thousands of dollars' worth of I.O.U.'s that he could not collect from his various lottery agencies throughout the state. His stores were also doing badly. He had bought much on credit—and in turn had been forced to give extensive credit in order to keep his goods turning over.

Furthermore, his paper was losing money. He was finally

forced to sell all—the paper, his stores and even his house. With what little cash he was able to salvage, he set out once again (this time with his wife and his newborn daughter, Caroline) for New York.

The winter of 1834-1835 was a bad one for Barnum. He read the want ads every day, looking for some sort of opportunity that he felt would suit his talents. Finally, for the little family was fast running out of grocery and rent money, he took a job selling hats and caps on commission.

He was almost at his wits' end when he got an unexpected windfall. A few of his old customers in Bethel paid up their debts, and with the few hundred dollars he received he opened a small grocery store on South Street, near the fish wharves, in partnership with a man named John Moody.

Now at last he was back in business for himself, but only in the smallest way. He was no better off than he had been nearly ten years before. Even his tremendous ego began to wither, and he almost lost faith in the ultimate destiny that he had always believed would be his.

3
George Washington's Nanny

COLEY BERTRAM was a friend and neighbor who always stopped by Barnum's store, whenever he was in the big city. One day in July, 1835, as the two talked over old times, Coley began telling a story about "George Washington's nanny."

Bertram had recently been part owner of an old Negro slave, Joice Heth, who was supposed on reliable authority to be one hundred and sixty-one years old. As if that didn't make her enough of a curiosity, she claimed that she had been George Washington's nurse when he was a baby! Bertram and his partner, R. W. Lindsay of Jefferson County, Kentucky, had been exhibiting the old woman in Philadelphia's Masonic Hall. But Bertram, not being of a show-business turn of mind, had sold out his share. Furthermore, he told P. T., Lindsay was anxious to sell out and go home.

As his friend talked, ideas began to buzz in Barnum's head. Maybe this ancient woman was just the pot of gold that he had been looking for!

P. T. Barnum hardly noticed Bertram leave the store. His mind was already in Philadelphia. And the next day he was on the train heading there.

Barnum had never seen—nor even imagined—a human being like Joice Heth. She looked like a living mummy, and might as well have been one thousand years old as one hundred and sixty-one. She lay on a high lounge in the middle of the room with her skeletonlike legs drawn up so that her knees were elevated two feet above the rest of her body. She was blind, her eyeballs so deeply sunken in their sockets that they seemed to have disappeared altogether. She hadn't a tooth in her mouth, and her head was covered by a thick bush of gray hair. Her left arm was drawn closely across her chest and the nails of the hand were four inches or more in length. Her right arm was the only part of her body that she could move.

But for all her physical handicaps, Joice's mind was keen and alert, and she talked loquaciously and clearly. When she was not speaking, she sang hymns and spirituals.

Her favorite topic of conversation, naturally, was George Washington. She told Barnum that she had been a house slave of Augustine Washington, and had been present at George's birth. In fact, she declared proudly, she had been the first person to put a diaper and shirt on "dear little Georgie," and had raised him throughout his early childhood as his nanny.

Barnum asked Lindsay for proof of the old slave's age and was shown a yellow bill of sale from Augustine Washington of Westmoreland County, Virginia, to Elizabeth Atwood of "one negro woman, named Joice Heth, aged fifty-four years, for and in consideration of thirty-three pounds lawful money of Virginia." It was dated February 5, 1727, and duly witnessed by William Washington and Richard Buckner.

Lindsay explained that Elizabeth Atwood was a sister-in-law of Augustine Washington and lived on a neighboring plantation—and that Joice, having long been the Washington family nurse, had been "borrowed back" by the Washingtons at George's birth in 1732. This story was gleefully confirmed by Joice herself.

Only one thing bothered Barnum. In one of his many biographies he recalls: "I enquired why the existence of such an extraordinary old woman had not been discovered long ago. Mr. Lindsay replied that she had been lying in an out-building of John S. Bowling, of Kentucky, for many years; that no one knew or seemed to care how old she was; that she had been taken from Virginia to Kentucky a long time ago; that the fact of her extreme age had but recently been brought to light by the discovery of this old paper in the Record Office in Westmoreland County by Mr. Bowling's son; and that he had become convinced that the document applied to his father's old slave, who was therefore really one hundred and sixty-one years of age." When confronted with the paper, Joice herself had confirmed the fact that she had actually been George Washington's nurse.

Barnum was convinced—probably because he wanted to be convinced—and then came the question of money. Lindsay's asking price was $3,000, but since he was dickering with the slickest horse trader in Connecticut, he finally settled for $1,000 to be paid within ten days. Barnum put down a small deposit to clinch the deal. Then he hurried back to New York to raise the rest of the money.

At this point, Barnum's total cash assets amounted to only $500. But he fast-talked a friend into lending him the other $500, sold out his interest in the store to Mr. Moody for expense money, and rushed down to Philadelphia to take title to his property. Now, although he was opposed to slavery, he became a slave-owner.

Barnum went to work with all the slothfulness of a Kansas cyclone sweeping across the prairie. Niblo's Garden, at Broadway and Prince Street, was New York's most popular saloon and refreshment center. It was large, open and airy, with an orchestra and what today would be called a "floor show." The central garden was surrounded by alcoves where guests could be seated and served. Niblo's, thought Barnum, was the perfect place to exhibit his ancient human relic.

William Niblo liked the idea, but he had no wish to show Joice Heth in his main garden, where her presence might be offensive to his more squeamish clientele. So he provided a room off the garden proper which was easily accessible to all his customers. Niblo agreed to furnish the room and lighting, pay for all advertising promotion, and hire a ticket seller. In return, he was to receive one half of the receipts. It turned out to be one of the most profitable deals Niblo ever made. Soon, he and Barnum were splitting $1,500 a week.

Barnum opened his advertising campaign with newspaper ads set in large type replete with curlicues and woodcuts— a type face that Barnum popularized, and which to this day is known as "circus type."

The ads related the story of the amazing Joice Heth— and reproduced a facsimile of the bill of sale that proved her authenticity. Barnum plastered New York with posters and produced a pamphlet that told the history of the ancient slave in far greater detail—and perhaps with a little more inventiveness—than did the ads. The pamphlet sold for six cents.

Within a week all New York was talking about the remarkable Aunt Joice, as Barnum called her. On opening day, the display room was crowded, and a long line of customers had formed before the ticket office.

P. T. had emphasized that Aunt Joice was a devout Baptist, and he invited the city's leading ministers to discuss the Scriptures with her, and to join her in singing hymns. The patronage of the clergy tended to give the exhibition an aspect of historical and religious significance, and drew many customers whose strict Puritan codes would not have allowed them to indulge in mere frivolous entertainment.

The show usually opened with either Barnum or his assistant—a shrewd and eloquent ex-lawyer named Levi Lyman—telling the dramatic story of how Joice's existence was discovered, and displaying Augustine Washington's bill of sale. They would then question the old woman about her relationship with George Washington and her answers about "little Georgie" were always clear, concise, and spoken with an air of loving nostalgia.

Then the questioning was thrown open to the audience. Some of the questions from spectators were deliberately designed to catch the old woman up in conflicting answers, but she never failed to come back with ready and sometimes witty replies that "never deviated," as Barnum later said, "from what had every evidence of being a plain, unvarnished statement of facts."

Frequently she asked the spectators to join her in singing the old religious songs, and quite often when they forgot the lines she filled them in. Nearly everyone who had come to the exhibit as a Doubting Thomas departed as a True Believer.

Nothing so sensational and newsworthy had happened in New York in years, and the Joice Heth story received daily press coverage.

"Auntie," a reporter said one day when he found her contentedly puffing away on a corncob pipe, "they say that smoking tobacco stunts your growth and shortens your life. How long have *you* been a smoker?"

"One hundred and twenty years, young man," the old lady replied with a toothless grin, "and it don't 'pear to have hurt me none." All New York laughed delightedly at the story when it appeared in the *Evening Star*.

The exhibit at Niblo's Garden continued to play to capacity houses for several months, and when the box office trade began to taper off—as it does eventually with any hit show—P. T. took Joice Heth on the road. He went first to Providence and then to Boston. The exhibition was preceded in both cities by Barnum's usual barrage of newspaper ads and handbills. And in both cities Aunt Joice was as tremendous a hit as she had been in New York.

One Boston reporter, temporarily overcome by his own mastery of language, wrote: "It *re-joice-heth* us exceedingly to know that we shall be permitted to look upon this old patriarch."

Then, when Boston attendance began to taper off, a letter to the editor appeared in Boston's leading paper. It stated that Joice Heth was a humbug—but the most curious and interesting humbug that had ever been devised.

"The fact is," the letter went on, "Joice Heth is not a human being at all. What purports to be a remarkably old woman is simply a curiously constructed automaton, made up of whalebone, India rubber and numberless springs ingeniously put together and made to move at the slightest touch according to the will of the operator. The exhibitor is a ventriloquist, and all the conversations apparently held with the old lady are purely imaginary." The letter was signed *"A Visitor."*

As a result, business skyrocketed again. Hundreds who hadn't seen the ancient Negro now came for a look at this amazing piece of machinery; while hundreds more who had already visited the exhibit wanted a second look to decide for themselves whether or not they had been fooled the first time around.

Barnum never admitted it, but there is little doubt that he was the writer of the "Visitor" letter.

Then, on exhibit again in New York, Joice Heth became seriously ill. Barnum sent her at once to the home of his brother Philo in Bethel, in charge of a free Negro woman whom he had hired in Boston as her nurse. There she was provided with the best of medical care; but on February 19, 1836, she died, and her remains were brought to New York in Philo's sleigh.

Some months before, an eminent New York surgeon, Dr. David L. Rogers, had seen Joice Heth on exhibit, and had been convinced that she was, in truth, as old as Barnum claimed. At that time he had asked permission to perform a postmortem on her body if she died while in Barnum's custody. P. T. had agreed and now, remembering his promise, he informed Dr. Rogers that he could proceed with his examination.

The postmortem took place in the presence of a number of physicians, medical students, clergymen and reporters. And the results, at least to Barnum, were electrifying. To a lesser degree, Dr. Rogers himself was astounded. He had expected the arteries around Joice's heart to be hardened almost to the point of ossification. Instead, their condition proved that the old woman, far from being one hundred and sixty-one, was probably not over eighty.

Barnum protested—as he continued to do for the rest of his life—that he had bought the old slave and exhibited her in good faith, relying on her appearance and the evidence of the antique Washington bill of sale. The doctor agreed that her appearance actually did indicate extreme old age and suggested that the papers had been forged and artificially aged, or else that they had applied to another of Augustine Washington's slaves.

Barnum, however, wondered how had the old woman become so familiar with the intimate details of the Washingtons' family life? He finally concluded that it was Lindsay who had swindled him.

He took Aunt Joice's remains back to Bethel, where he gave her a Christian burial.

4

Bad Luck on the Circus Trail

Upon the death of Joice Heth, Phineas Taylor Barnum was at loose ends again. Most of the money he had made had somehow slipped through his fingers. But he still held on to the belief that his future lay somewhere in show business.

After about two months of scouting around for something that he considered worthy of his talents, he finally signed with Aaron Turner's Traveling Circus as ticket seller, secretary and treasurer, and part-time ringmaster. Barnum was to receive $80 a month plus one-fifth of the profits.

Sending Charity and Caroline back to Bethel, P. T. started from Danbury with the Turner show on April 26, 1836. The circus traveled over the rutted country dirt roads in four wagons, and played dozens of little towns in New

England, New York, New Jersey, Delaware, Pennsylvania, Maryland, Virginia and North Carolina. The talent consisted of Turner's two sons, who were trick riders; Joe Pentland, one of America's first great clowns; and a juggler. There was also, of course, a small brass band that made up in volume what it lacked in musical skill.

During his months with Turner, Barnum kept his eyes and ears constantly open, learning all the tricks of the trade that he was later to put to such profitable use. He also began to develop an attitude toward show business that was to become almost a religion. He abhorred the Puritanical attitudes that looked upon entertainment as evil. He knew deep down that people needed an outlet for their gayer, happier moods. And he felt that to provide it was a worthy and honorable calling.

Barnum attended church regularly on Sundays. One morning, in a small Maryland town where the show happened to be playing, the minister's sermon consisted of a violent and abusive tirade against circuses and everything and everybody associated with them.

After the preaching, Barnum strode to the floor of the pulpit and addressed the congregation for half an hour on the rights of humans to amuse and be amused. Although the minister repeatedly interrupted Barnum and ordered the people to leave, the congregation stayed and listened attentively to all that Barnum had to say.

"I told them," he later said in relating the incident, "that while we made no great pretense of religion, we were not the worst people in the world, and that we felt entitled to at least decent treatment when we went to hear the preaching of the Gospel."

When his six-month contract with Turner came to an end in October, P. T. found himself $1,200 to the good.

With this money he bought two or three wagons and started out on his own.

Road-showing a traveling circus was fun for Barnum. It carried him back to his carefree boyhood. But, financially, it was a losing proposition. He took on several partners during the next year and a half and at one point even chartered a showboat to play the Mississippi River towns. But in the end, after two years as itinerant showman, he finally gave up, disbanded what was left of his company, and went back to New York.

For a while Barnum settled down to the mundane job of writing ads for the Broadway Amphitheater at a salary of $4 a week. However, his advertising job brought him into contact with several of New York's leading newspapermen—many of whom remembered and admired him from the rambunctious days of his Joice Heth promotion—and he managed to supplement his meager income by writing articles for the Sunday editions.

It was while he was idly looking over the papers one afternoon to check on his Amphitheater ads that he came across a news item that put him back into show business.

5
The Lamb Who Sheared the Wolves

THE news story that caught Barnum's eye that routine afternoon was a report that the "collection of curiosities" comprising Scudder's American Museum was up for sale. The asking price was $15,000, although as far as Barnum's finances at the moment were concerned it might as well have been $15,000,000. Just the same, the story started big ideas scrambling over each other in P. T.'s mind, and his heart began to pound the way it had the day Coley Bertram first told him about Joice Heth.

Barnum had visited the museum a number of times in his off hours, and to his showman's eyes it was a deadly bore. But he had often idly speculated upon how his own flair for showmanship could turn it into the kind of spectacular amusement center that New Yorkers would stand in line to buy tickets for. He decided that somehow Scudder's American Museum was going to be *Barnum's* American Museum.

John Scudder had founded the American Museum in 1810, the year of Barnum's birth. Slowly he had built it up from a hodgepodge of stuffed animals and musty historic relics until now, in 1841, it was a dust-ridden collection of doodads, whatnots and oddities, housed in a large stone building on the corner of Broadway and Ann Street in the heart of bustling and fast-growing New York.

To his stuffed animals and reptiles, dusty military flags and uniforms, rusty guns and other curiosities, Scudder had added such attractions as a portrait gallery of famous Americans, a collection of wax figures, cracked and moldy models of Jerusalem and Paris, trained dogs, live snakes and alligators, and a midget. There was always a down-at-the-heels "Professor" on hand who lectured on scientific and geographic subjects that were usually over the heads of the paying customers.

Over the years, Mr. Scudder had amassed a considerable fortune from the museum, and its contents were said to be worth in excess of $50,000. After his death, the ownership descended to his daughters, and they turned the museum's management over to John Heath, the administrator of their father's estate. Business began to go rapidly downhill, and the Scudder girls decided to sell out for whatever they could get. Heath advised that $15,000 was the most they could hope for on the basis of a quick sale.

It didn't take Barnum long to ferret out these basic facts once the idea of buying Scudder's took hold of him. And his brains immediately went into high gear to figure out ways and means of pulling off the deal. One evening, on meeting a friend, he blurted out: "I see that Scudder's Museum is for sale. And I'm going to buy it."

Knowing that P. T. was hard put to buy meat for the family stewpot, the friend grinned. *"You?* What do you intend buying it with?"

"Well, sir," Barnum declared confidently, "I don't have any gold or silver. So I'm going to buy it with *brass."*

And it was purest Yankee brass—combined with all the horse-trading tricks that he had learned the hard way—that finally put Barnum's name up in lights over the big museum.

Since the building in which Scudder's collection was housed belonged to a rich retired merchant named Francis W. Olmstead, he seemed to be the logical man to contact first. But how to make the contact was a problem, since Barnum was acquainted with no one who had direct access to him. After thinking it over from every angle, P. T. finally concluded that the best approach was the direct Yankee peddler approach. He sat down and carefully composed a letter so frank, so open, so honest—and, above all, so bold—that he felt sure it would arouse the great man's curiosity.

Barnum wrote that he wanted to purchase the contents of the Scudder Museum—but that, since he had no money, *he wanted Mr. Olmstead to buy it for him!*

He figured that this opening would be enough to cause the elderly financier to sit up and take notice of the brassy young man who had the nerve to propose it—as indeed it did.

His idea, Barnum explained, was that he would buy back the collection from Mr. Olmstead on the installment plan, paying a reasonable rate of interest, and that he would also pick up the lease on the building. He was sure, he went on, that his past experience in catering to the entertainment needs of the public would assure success for the venture, and he promised that he would devote all of his time, energy and talents to the business.

"You may bind me in any way," he wrote, "as tightly as you please. I only ask you to give me a chance to dig out or scratch out—and if at any time I fail to meet the installment due, I will vacate the premises and forfeit all that I may have paid you to that date."

He declared his determination to devote every dollar of the net profits to paying back his obligation—requesting only that he be allowed to retain $12.50 a week with which to support his family.

P. T. shrewdly added the suggestion that by making such an arrangement, Mr. Olmstead would have a permanent tenant for the building—whereas otherwise the museum would very likely be closed in the near future.

Barnum took the letter to Mr. Olmstead's house in Park Place and handed it to the butler. He had a reply in two days. Mr. Olmstead would talk with him.

Olmstead received him with a show of aristocratic politeness, and then got down to business. Eyeing P. T. closely, he began asking searching questions about his background. Barnum told him about his boyhood in Bethel, his youthful business ventures, and finally, in greater detail, his experiences in show business.

Through it all, the old gentleman maintained an austere expression. But Barnum was able to perceive that he was more than just a little bit intrigued by his unorthodox business proposition.

Barnum didn't put it quite that way when he told about the meeting in his autobiography. "I thought I could see the good, open-hearted noble *man* peering through his eyes," he wrote.

But it amounted to the same thing. No man in Mr. Francis Olmstead's day ever got to be a millionaire by being too open-hearted and noble.

After listening to Barnum's story, Mr. Olmstead asked: "Who can you give me for references?"

"Any man in my line," Barnum replied. He named William Niblo, Edmund Simpson (manager of the Park Theater), and Moses Yale Beach, a go-getting newspaperman who had recently bought the New York *Sun* and quickly made it into one of New York's most influential papers.

"Will any of them call on me?" Olmstead asked.

"I'm sure they will be glad to," Barnum replied. It was arranged that P. T.'s references would call the next day— and that Barnum could expect Mr. Olmstead's verdict the day after that.

Happy to be of service to a likable young man who in their opinion was destined to "go places," Beach, Niblo, Simpson and several others Barnum had named drove to Park Place and had personal talks with Olmstead. The following morning, on schedule, Barnum himself showed up to hear Mr. Olmstead's verdict.

"Mr. Barnum," the old gentleman began brusquely, "I don't like your references."

For one of the few times in his life, Barnum was at a momentary loss for words. Then Olmstead burst out laughing. "They all speak too well of you," he said. "They talk as if they were partners of yours and intended to share in the profits."

Finally, the laugh done with, the two got down to specifics. It was agreed that Olmstead would retain title to the museum's contents until they were paid for; that the rent would be $3,000 a year on a lease of ten years; and that Olmstead would appoint—at Barnum's expense—an accountant and ticket-taker who would render the landlord a weekly statement of the box-office receipts.

By this time Barnum's head was riding in the clouds; his wild dreams were coming true. Then Olmstead threw him a curve.

"I think you are going to make a success of this, young fellow," he said, "but sound business methods demand that I have some kind of solid security—bonds, perhaps, or unemcumbered real estate."

Barnum owned no bonds—and the one or two pieces of property that he still held title to in Connecticut were mortgaged. For a moment he felt his happy cloudland begin to burst. Then he remembered something. His eyes lit up as his mind raced back to a sunny afternoon in a Bethel hayfield—and the small-boy disappointment when his fabled Ivy Island estate had turned out to be nothing more than a five-acre piece of snake-infested swamp.

Now it was his turn to throw a fast curve at Mr. Olmstead—a harmless one, he reasoned, since it had been a gag in the first place.

"Well, sir," he said after an instant's hesitation, "I *do* happen to own five acres of land in the midst of fine farming country up in Connecticut. And it is free and clear of any mortgages or liens."

Olmstead smiled, seemingly satisfied. "Fine! Fine!" he said. "May I ask what you paid for it?"

"It was a gift, sir, from my late grandfather, Phineas Taylor, given to me on account of my name."

"Was he a rich man?"

"He was considered well off in those parts," Barnum replied truthfully.

"Then it is doubtless valuable . . ." Olmstead ventured.

You ought to see it! Barnum thought to himself.

"And I suppose you would not like to part with it, considering that it was so personal a present."

P. T. smiled, sure now of the ground he stood on. "I will never have to do that," he said earnestly. "I fully intend to make my payments to you punctually until my debt is paid in full."

"That's the spirit!" said Mr. Olmstead. "I think I will make the purchase for you. At all events, I will think it over. Meanwhile, I suggest that you see the administrator of the Scudder estate and get his best terms. I plan to be out of town for a few days, so meet me here again in a week."

Barnum hurried at once across town to the office of John Heath, the Scudder administrator.

"Fifteen thousand dollars is the price," Mr. Heath said firmly.

"I will give you ten thousand," P. T. countered. "Payable in seven equal installments and backed by gilt-edge security."

"I couldn't think of selling at that price," Heath insisted.

"May I see you again tomorrow after I have talked with my principals?"

"Certainly," Heath said. "But my price still will be fifteen thousand and not a copper less."

Maybe John Heath had never dealt with a Connecticut Yankee trader before. Before the week was out, Barnum had made a deal to buy the collection for $12,000—payment to be made and possession to be given on November 15, 1841.

But when Heath arrived at Olmstead's office on the morning of November 15, his first words rocked Barnum on his heels.

"I'm sorry, gentlemen," Heath said, "but I cannot proceed any further in this case. I have just sold Scudder's to the directors of Peale's Museum for fifteen thousand dollars and have received their check for one thousand in advance."

Barnum protested that they had already made an agreement.

Heath shrugged his shoulders. "We had nothing in writing," he declared. "And I felt that it was my duty to do the best I could for Mr. Scudder's orphaned girls."

"I'm sorry, too, Barnum," Mr. Olmstead said. "But my hands are tied. You were a risk—although a good one, I had decided—but now I have a permanent tenant for my building without becoming financially involved myself."

So everybody was sorry! Barnum thought. A whale of a lot of good that did P. T. Barnum! So he was licked! Well, he had been licked before. Bowing slightly to the two gentlemen—and to his own dismal bad luck—he turned and left the room.

But Taylor Barnum was never one to stay licked very long. And when his dander had cooled off a little he sat down to think things out. Somewhere, his trader's sixth sense kept telling him, there was a rat hiding in the woodwork.

Why, he asked himself, did the Peale brothers want to buy a big museum of curiosities in New York—and where had they raked up all that money in such a hurry? Barnum knew, for a starter, that Charles Willson Peale—the famous American artist who was best known for his several por- traits of George Washington—had opened a small museum in his studio in Philadelphia shortly after the Revolution. Its contents consisted mostly of portraits, with a few natural history objects thrown in. On his death he had passed it along to his sons—Rembrandt, Titian, and Raphael Peale—who had kept the studio-museum open in a half- hearted way. But these men were artists, not showmen— and they had maintained the little museum more or less in memory of their father.

Barnum's extra-large lump of curiosity began to itch. There must be an answer someplace. And the logical place to begin looking for it was through his newspaper friends— notably Moses Y. Beach of the *Sun,* and James Gordon Bennett, the fire-eating owner of the New York *Herald.*

With their help, but mainly through his own energetic digging, P. T. soon unearthed the facts. A group of specu- lators, headed by a discredited ex-bank president, had bought the little Peale collection for next to nothing. They then planned to announce the merger of Peale's Museum with the American Museum, thus capitalizing on the highly honored and reputable Peale name—and at the same time issue and sell stock in the new enterprise to the public in the amount of $50,000. With this money they would pay Heath his remaining $14,000, pocket the rest, make them- selves scarce, and leave the hapless stockholders holding the empty bag.

Armed with his evidence, Barnum went at once to Beach, Bennett, and several other of his friends among New York's newspaper editors and told them the whole sordid story.

"If you will grant me the use of your columns," he said to them, "I will blow this crooked speculation sky-high."

Always eager for a good crusade, especially when it involved a juicy scandal that would sell extra papers, the editors happily agreed. And, beginning the next day, Barnum began flooding the city's news columns with dozens of eye-popping stories about the proposed swindle. He cited facts and figures and named names—assuring his readers that buying stock in such an outrageous scheme would be the same as wrapping up their hard-earned money in neat packages and throwing it in the East River.

As a result of P. T.'s endless outpouring of newspaper reports, the would-be swindlers sold not a dollar's worth of stock. "When I got through with them," Barnum later gloated, "the stock was as dead as a herring!"

To all his friends who mentioned the museum to him, P. T. simply stated that he had lost his chance to buy it. But he knew very well what was coming, and he prepared for it by arranging a confidential meeting with Mr. Heath.

"When are the directors of the new museum company due to pay the remaining fourteen thousand dollars?" he wanted to know.

"On the 26th day of December," Heath replied. "Otherwise they will forfeit their original thousand-dollar deposit."

"I assure you they will never pay it," Barnum said, "for the simple reason that they won't be able to raise that amount. Then you will find the museum collection on your hands again."

Mr. Heath was doubtful. "They won't want to lose their deposit," he protested.

"I am planning to leave for the South with an exhibition," Barnum declared, his tongue firmly pressed against his cheek and his fingers crossed. "And once I get started I would not touch the museum at any price. But if you will agree with me, in strictest confidence, that in case these gentlemen do not pay you as agreed on December 26th, I may have it on the 27th for twelve thousand, then I will take the risk and stay in New York until that date."

"That is a fair proposal," Mr. Heath assented.

"Very well," Barnum continued, "all I ask of you is that this arrangement between the two of us shall not be mentioned to anyone."

Heath nodded his agreement.

"Then at 10 A.M., on December 27th, I wish you to meet me at Mr. Olmstead's apartment prepared to sign the museum's contents over to me. Provided, naturally, that you are not paid your promised fourteen thousand dollars on the 26th."

Mr. Heath agreed—and at Barnum's request he put the deal in writing.

Barnum went to see Mr. Olmstead and told him of his meeting with Heath. The old financier, too, promised secrecy. He sensed that this young Barnum had an extra ace or two up his sleeve. And he was eager to find out what it was. He smiled as he remembered the long-ago days of his own youth, when he himself was getting a start in business by pulling some surprises.

About the first week in December Barnum received a letter from the Peale's Museum group of confidence men—who now called themselves the New York Museum. If he would be kind enough to meet with their board of directors on the following Monday, the letter said, he would probably hear something to his advantage.

Barnum had known all along that this would happen—

just as he had known years before that he could sell worthless green bottles and rusty tinware in Keeler & Whitlock's
country store. Because of his newspaper articles, the group
hadn't sold a single share of stock. They were powerless to
stop Barnum's editorial campaign. Therefore they would
buy his silence. It was as simple as that.

P. T. was punctual at the meeting, and the directors
greeted him with warmest regard. They said that they had
closely followed his show-business career, and that after
much discussion had come to the conclusion that he was
just the man they needed to manage the new combined
museum.

Like any good sucker is supposed to, Barnum professed
to be greatly complimented. When asked to mention a
salary, he specified $3,000 a year. The directors agreed.
His salary, they said, would begin on January 1.

As he was going out of the door, the genial old ex-banker
remarked as if in passing: "Of course, Mr. Barnum, we
will see no more of your articles in the papers."

Barnum smiled the grateful smile of a shorn lamb. "I
always try to serve the interest of my employers," he said.

Now that they had silenced Barnum, the directors re-
laxed. They knew that no one else would try to buy the
American Museum, and they decided not to try to sell any
more stock until after the first of January—by which time
they were sure that the public would have forgotten all about
Barnum's attacks. As for their agreement to pay Mr.
Heath his $14,000 by December 26, they figured that he
would happily wait until it suited their pleasure to make
the payment. This detail bothered them so little, in fact, that
they did not call on Heath at all on December 26—nor

did they even take the trouble to write a note of explanation for not doing so.

Promptly at 10 A.M. on the 27th, Barnum met with Messrs. Heath and Olmstead, and their attorneys, and the papers making Barnum sole owner of the American Museum were duly signed, sealed and delivered.

But Barnum had too much ham actor in his soul to resist a curtain line.

His first official act as owner was to write and mail the following note:

AMERICAN MUSEUM, New York
December 27, 1841

To the President and Directors of the New York Museum:
Gentlemen: It gives me great pleasure to inform you that you are placed upon the Free List of this establishment until further notice.

P. T. BARNUM, Proprietor

6

"The Prince of Humbugs"

Now that he had so deftly flimflammed the confidence men who had been all set to flimflam *him,* Barnum at once got down to the serious business of remaking the American Museum to his own design.

The fact that he had gone into debt up to his neck to buy property that had been a money-loser for years "made him no never-mind," as the folks up Bethel way would say. He knew exactly what kind of showplace the museum should be, and could be—and he was supremely confident that in no time at all he could start keeping its books in black ink instead of red. In the first place, P. T. was a master of all the tricks of the showman's trade—an art that neither Scudder, nor any other museum owner, had ever bothered to learn. And when he had need for a new trick he could always concoct one.

As a modest starter, he reopened the American Museum at *sunrise* on New Year's Day 1842—a custom that was continued as long as the museum remained in business. Each morning the doors were thrown open to the public as soon as the first rays of the rising sun began slanting up over Brooklyn. This unusual opening hour became so well known throughout the country that, as Barnum later wrote, "Strangers coming to the city would often take a tour through my halls before going to breakfast or to their hotels."

As fast as he could round them up, Barnum began to add what he referred to as "transient novelties" to his permanent exhibits. These consisted of trained-flea circuses, trick dogs, dwarfs, giants, fat people, knife throwers, dancers, magicians, Punch-and-Judy shows (the first ever seen in the United States), live wild animals in cages, and European glassblowers who fashioned such delicate little trinkets as deer and birds, which they sold to the spectators.

Most of these added attractions were authentic; many were exaggerated in his advertising and outdoor posters; and some were what P. T. candidly called "claptrap." But each one was designed as a magnet to entice the price of admission out of passersby.

To accommodate these live shows, Barnum began enlarging the small musty Lecture Room, in which Mr. Scudder's "professors" had delivered their dull dissertations, until in later years the room became one of the largest and finest theaters in New York.

As a result of Barnum's tireless efforts business began to boom, and before long the museum was showing a healthy profit. Barnum stuck steadfastly to his original financial plans. Except for $600 a year to support his family, he plowed all of his profits back into advertising and promotion—and to paying off his debt to Mr. Olmstead.

One day at noon, a few months after Barnum had taken over, Olmstead happened into the office and saw the boss lunching on a cold meat sandwich.

"Is this the way you always eat your dinner?" the financier wanted to know.

"Yes, sir," Barnum replied seriously. "Except on the Sabbath I have never eaten a warm dinner since I purchased the museum. And I never intend to do so until I am out of debt."

This was the kind of talk Mr. Olmstead liked to hear. "In that case," he predicted, "you will pay for the museum before the year is out."

Actually, Barnum took a year and a half to pay off his mortgage. But by far the greater part of his profits during that time went into advertising and promotional stunts.

Phineas Taylor Barnum was the great-granddaddy of American advertising. He knew its tremendous power, and he spared not a drop of printer's ink to make Barnum's American Museum the talk of New York. Partly because of his lavish expenditures in their advertising columns, and partly because many of his outlandish exploits were sensational news in themselves, most of the New York papers saw to it that his name was rarely missing from their news columns.

Barnum made no bones about the fact that much of his flood of printed advertising—and most of the pictures of his curiosities—were downright hokum. But he also knew that his customers got much more value than the modest cost of their tickets. Most of them went away with the desire to come back again and bring their friends.

P. T. gloried in the title "The Prince of Humbugs,"

which he himself had arranged to have his newspaper friends bestow upon him. He knew that people enjoyed being "taken in" now and then, along with being genuinely entertained by his legitimate offerings.

He kept a brass band on the museum's front balcony to provide what his advertisements proclaimed as "Free Music for the Millions." New Yorkers flocked to Broadway and Ann Street to enjoy the concerts Barnum was giving for nothing. But the old master made sure that his band was composed of the worst and noisiest musicians he could find, and the crowds fled into the relative quiet of the museum to avoid having to listen.

"When people expect something for nothing," Barnum observed sagely, "they are sure to be cheated, and rightfully deserve to be."

P. T.'s head was always full of promotion ideas. Sometimes he planned them painstakingly in advance. But often they turned up by accident, and when this happened he put them to work almost by instinct.

For example:

One morning, a large, healthy-looking man showed up at the box office begging for the price of a meal. When Barnum inquired why he wasn't working, the man replied that he had been unable to find a job, and would be willing to do anything to earn some money.

Barnum gave him a quarter. "Go get yourself a good breakfast," he said, "and when you come back I will give you an easy job at a dollar and a half a day."

When the man returned, Barnum handed him five ordinary building bricks.

"Now," he said, "go and lay a brick on the sidewalk at the corner of Broadway and Ann Street. Lay another one close by the Museum; a third at the corner of Broadway and Vesey Street; and a fourth in front of the church. Then, carrying your fifth brick in your hand, make the full circuit again and exchange a brick at every point. Understand?"

The puzzled man didn't, and stood there scratching his head. "What's it all about?"

"It's just a little fun," Barnum explained. "But do your work faithfully. Keep as deaf as a post and shrug off any questions that anyone might ask you. Then, at the end of every hour, walk up to the ticket office, show this ticket and go in. Walk through every hall in the building, then pass out and start laying your bricks all over again."

At the end of the first hour the sidewalks in front of the building were jammed with curious lookers-on. And when the "bricklayer" presented the ticket, several dozen people bought tickets and followed him inside to see what was going on. Every hour, for several days, the workman carried on his silly task of laying down bricks and picking them up again. And every time he went into the museum, he was followed by a crowd of paying customers.

Finally, after a few days of this tomfoolery, the policeman on the beat went to Barnum for an explanation. Barnum told him the story, and the officer laughed.

"Just the same, Mr. Barnum," he said, "you'll have to call your man off. He's tying up the traffic on my beat."

Naturally, the story made the papers. "And," said Barnum, "it materially advanced my purpose of making the museum a lively place."

On the Fourth of July, six months after his opening, Barnum decided to do a little extra something in the way of a patriotic gesture. The obvious thing seemed to be to hang a string of American flags across the street, since such a display would surely attract the attention of thousands of people who would be passing the museum that day with plenty of holiday leisure time and loose money in their pockets. The only trouble was that St. Paul's Church stood directly opposite the museum, and there was nothing to attach the other end of his flag rope to but one of the tall trees in the churchyard.

When he approached the church vestrymen for permission to do this, they called the whole idea a sacrilege, and flatly refused. Nevertheless, when P. T. returned to his office he ordered his workmen to have a string of flags made ready and, at sunrise on the Fourth, to attach one end to the third story of the museum and the other end to the top of a churchyard tree.

It didn't take long for two of St. Paul's vestrymen to come running across Broadway, their coattails flying, and storm Barnum's office.

"Let us keep cool, gentlemen," Barnum said soothingly. "Why don't we go out into the street and take another look at how really attractive the flags appear."

Out on the sidewalk, Barnum said, "Really, gentlemen, those flags look very beautiful, and they certainly do not harm your tree. I always stop my balcony music when you hold weekday services, and I think it is only fair that you return the favor."

By this time, one of the vestrymen was so angry that he shouted:

"If those flags are not taken down in ten minutes, I personally will *cut them down!*"

This was what Barnum had been waiting for. A large throng had gathered and now Barnum dramatically rolled up his sleeves and declared in stentorian tones:

"Well, mister, I would just like to see you dare to try to cut down the American flag on the Fourth of July! You must be a Britisher! But I'll show you a thousand pair of loyal Yankee hands in two minutes if you dare to take down the Stars and Stripes on this great birthday of American freedom!"

As if on cue, a big, brawny giant of a man pushed his way to the front of the crowd and stuck out his huge jaw.

"What's this John Bull talking about?" he roared. Then to the vestryman, who by this time was getting more than a little bit alarmed: "If you want to save a whole bone in your body, you'd better never talk again about hauling down the American flag in the city of New York!"

A menacing mutter began to run through the crowd and the vestrymen retreated to their church.

The next day Barnum's conscience began to bother him and he stepped over to St. Paul's and apologized for an incident that, he said, had apparently gotten out of hand. The churchmen, probably still a bit shaken by the experience of the day before, decided that it wouldn't hurt their trees or the dignity of St. Paul's if Mr. Barnum wanted to tie up a string of flags on any special occasions that might follow. And once again P. T. assured them that his discordant band would keep their instrument silenced whenever the church so requested.

Barnum's agile brain worked constantly at the endless task of sniffing out new and sensational curiosities and oddities. Some of his ideas sprang full-fledged out of his own imagination. Some were rarities that had existed unnoticed and unsung, alone in their own little spheres until Barnum came along to present them to the world at large. And some were born of Barnum's desire just to do something different.

As far as anyone knows, P. T. Barnum fathered that now-universal institution known as the baby show. The idea came to him one evening as he was playing with ten-year-old Caroline before her bedtime. *My! How pretty she was! And how bright for her age!* And at once the thought struck him that other parents must be as proud of their children as he and Charity were. Quickly he rushed over to his office to rough out the first Baby Show ad.

He planned and advertised the first show well in advance —not only to insure plenty of entries but also to give the newspapers time to build it up in their news columns. There were to be prizes for the most beautiful girl baby, the handsomest boy baby, the brightest baby, the most look-alike twins—and many other categories.

The baby shows were such fantastic successes that he followed them up with dog shows, pet shows, and poultry shows. And from all of them the money came rolling in.

In spite of his large expenditures for new talent and sales gimmicks—or, more probably, because of them— money came pouring through the museum box office in such vast quantities that Barnum was actually at a loss sometimes to figure out ways and means of carrying out his original plan of plowing back all first-year profits into advertising and promotion. He intended, as he said, to "sow first and reap later."

Then, as always happened when he needed it, an idea struck him that was truly grandiose.

At tremendous cost, he employed artists to paint large oval portraits of every important animal known to zoologists—enough painting so that one could be placed between every pair of windows around the entire museum. He also installed powerful calcium lights—the first ever seen in New York—across the whole top of the building.

When the paintings were ready, he had workmen put

them all up in a single night. The effect on the public when people first saw them the next morning was as if a whole new world of wonders had sprung up by some kind of magic between the darkness of one day and the sunrise of the next.

It was perhaps the greatest crowd-stopper in the history of show business. And when, at nightfall, the powerful light burst forth, they threw a flood of brilliance up and down Broadway from the Battery to Niblo's Garden "so bright that a man could see to read a newspaper in the street."

As Barnum described it:

"I never before saw so many open mouths and astonished eyes. Some people were puzzled to know what it all meant; some looked as if they thought it was an enchanted palace of some kind. Strangers would gape at this great pictorial magazine and argue that an establishment with so many animals on the outside must have something unusual going on inside. And in they would go to see. At all events, the museum receipts took a jump forward of nearly a hundred dollars a day, and they never fell back again."

Once he had them inside, Barnum went to great lengths to please and astonish the out-of-towners, and he gave them plenty of colored pictures to take back home with them. Tourists from as far away as the westernmost reaches of the Erie Canal solemnly advised friends never to visit New York without paying at least one visit to the fabulous showplace at the corner of Broadway and Ann Street.

In the early 1840's the great flood of migration from the settlements of the eastern seaboard to the fertile prairie lands of the West had already begun. To the city dwellers of the East, one of the most interesting aspects of the West was the presence there of the Plains Indians about whom so many hair-raising stories were told. It was inevitable that the idea of staging some kind of Indian show occurred to P. T. Barnum.

At the outset, he experimented with actors made up as Indians. But it quickly became evident that audiences were not interested in a make-believe wild west. So Barnum sent an agent to Iowa to find a real-live band of Sioux, which he imported to New York complete with interpreter.

The Sioux band—consisting of the biggest, most muscular braves and the handsomest squaws that the agent could round up—was wild and woolly enough to suit even the most critical museum patron. Not only could the Indians not speak a word of English but they had never seen a railroad train nor a steamboat. The sight of the huge conglomeration of streets and buildings that was New York, and the massive crowds of people, nearly threw them into a panic. But Barnum and their interpreter, himself a half-breed scout, managed to calm them down. Barnum installed them in large, airy rooms on the museum's top floor. There they managed to set up a Sioux-type village of sorts and lived as best they could in their tribal way.

When they had finally gotten used to their strange circumstances, they seemed to enjoy performing their ritualistic dances on the big stage with an audience out front. But they usually became so absorbed in their dancing, waving their lances and feathered tomahawks so realistically that it was dangerous for anyone except their interpreter to be on the stage with them. Often, after finishing their war dance, they would leap and peer about as if in search of victims for their scalping knives. After a few such performances, Barnum put up a strong rope barrier on the front of the stage between the dancers and the audience in the interests of avoiding an impromptu massacre.

After about a week, Barnum and the interpreter decided they had better stage a less bloodthirsty type of entertainment. The interpreter suggested the traditional Sioux Wedding Dance as a more tranquil, yet just as authentic, presentation.

However, before the first show, Barnum was informed that he would have to provide a new, red woolen blanket for the bridegroom to present to his prospective father-in-law. The blanket cost $10, and this seemed like a reasonable production cost—until Barnum was told that he must buy a new blanket for every performance. It did him no good to protest that the wedding was only stage make-believe. To the Indians, it was the real thing—and the old chief looked so menacing that Barnum was glad enough to provide the blankets as demanded. Since the show went on twice a day, six days a week, Barnum's blanket bill for the first week came to $120. He prudently decided to change once more to another type of peaceful, yet less expensive, dancing exhibit.

But the Indians wearied of their strange New York adventures and began to long for their normal way of life on the Great Plains. They became completely depressed when Do-humme, one of the most beautiful squaws, sickened for no apparent reason and died.

Barnum arranged for Do-humme to be buried with full tribal honors. After the required days of fasting and mourning had passed, the Sioux at last departed for the friendly Iowa prairies, and such familiar creatures as buffalos instead of clanging horsecars and shouting audiences.

7
The Fabulous Fiji Mermaid

ONE of the most preposterous humbugs in P. T. Barnum's long and lucrative career was the fantastic fraud of the monkey-faced mermaid from Fiji. Barnum knew that the mermaid was fake. It *had* to be! But from the moment he first gazed upon its repulsive features, his eyes saw it through a rosy haze of dollar signs.

In 1817, the captain of a New England clipper ship had bought it in Calcutta from a group of Japanese sailors who claimed to have caught it in their nets near the Fiji Islands and carefully embalmed it. The gullible Yankee was so impressed that he dipped into the ship's funds for $6,000 to pay for it, thinking that he would make himself rich by exhibiting his mermaid throughout the world.

The captain put his mermaid on exhibition for a short time in a dockside coffeehouse in London, but no one was interested. Then, disheartened, he took it back to Boston, put it in safekeeping and returned to the command of his old ship to pay off the $6,000 that he had appropriated from his employers to buy it. He died penniless, his entire estate consisting of the mermaid, which became his son's sole inheritance. The son sold it to Moses Kimball, proprietor of the Boston Museum.

Like all museum owners of that era, Kimball considered himself a sort of left-handed scientist rather than an out-and-out showman. After purchasing the mermaid, he decided that it was just a little bit too outlandish to go with his other musty but authentic displays, and so he took it down to New York to his old friend Barnum.

The creature, though repulsive to look at, was a real work of Oriental art. The upper part of its three-foot length was that of some sort of monkey. Its head and shoulders were covered thinly with dark hair; its eyes, mouth, ears, breasts, nipples, and even arms, hands and nails, were grotesquely humanoid in appearance.

The lower portion of the mermaid was that of a salmon-like fish. But the fish and the monkey had been so skillfully put together that the spine ran in an unbroken line from the fish tail to the base of the skull. It was impossible to tell just where the two halves were joined together. The hair of the monkey appeared to grow down several inches over the scales of the fish, and a close examination under a microscope revealed that tiny fish scales underlay almost all of the animal hair.

Shriveled and misshapen, its hands were thrown up over its ugly open mouth—the whole giving the impression that the creature had died in extreme agony.

After looking the thing over, his excitement growing all the time, Barnum called in a naturalist for his opinion.

The naturalist studied the mermaid for a while and shook his head in puzzlement.

"It can't be real," he said at last, "but for the life of me I can't imagine how it was manufactured. I never saw a monkey with such teeth, arms or hands, and I never saw a fish that had that peculiar kind of fins."

"Then why do you say that it was manufactured?" Barnum asked.

"Because I don't believe in mermaids."

"Then my reason is as good as yours," Barnum said firmly. "From now on, I'm going to believe in mermaids."

There had to be an extraordinary buildup for such an extraordinary curio. If he simply advertised it in a routine way and placed it on exhibition, the public would laugh it off as a more-than-usual piece of trickery and quickly forget about it.

No, the suckers would have to be really primed for this one! They'd have to be pushing one another out of line at the box office to get a look! The idea, Barnum finally decided, was to start the ball rolling some distance away.

Accordingly, a few weeks later, a news story appeared in the New York *Herald,* datelined Montgomery, Alabama, stating that a certain Dr. J. Griffin, a representative of the Lyceum of Natural History in London, England, had recently arrived in that city from Pernambuco, Brazil. The Montgomery correspondent stated that Dr. Griffin had in his possession a rare specimen of a genuine mermaid which had been captured in the waters around the Fiji Islands and which the doctor had purchased at a very high figure for the London Lyceum.

In a few days, another story about Dr. Griffin and his remarkable mermaid made the New York papers. This one came from Charleston, South Carolina. It was followed by another story of the same nature from Washington, D. C., stating that Dr. Griffin had some business to attend to in both Philadelphia and New York before returning to London.

In Philadelphia, local editors begged the favor of seeing the mermaid for themselves, and Dr. Griffin, stating that he was sure the Lyceum directors could not possibly object, granted their request. Apparently the Philadelphia reporters were completely taken in, for the next day the papers were full of the mermaid story.

During the buildup, Barnum had prepared pictures of the mermaid—pictures that depicted her as a beautiful woman with a fish's tail, perched on a coral rock combing her flowing hair. He sent the pictures to the New York papers along with a news release. The release stated that he had hoped to be able to show the mermaid in his museum, but that the Lyceum in London would not permit it. Anyhow, here were the pictures just in case the editors could use them.

When Dr. Griffin arrived in New York with his mermaid and registered at the Pacific Hotel on Greenwich Street, he was besieged by reporters. Like the newspapermen in Philadelphia, the New York reporters seemed convinced that the mermaid from Fiji was real, and their reports to the public were, to use Barnum's phrase, "quite satisfactory."

Barnum had been somewhat worried that the New York reporters might recognize Dr. J. Griffin as Levi Lyman, the man who had worked with him on the Joice Heth promotion, and he breathed a sigh of relief when Dr. Griffin's scholarly English-scientist facade fooled them completely.

Barnum had also written a pamphlet about the mermaid, complete with pictures, and put it on sale at the Newsstands of all principal hotels and stores at a penny each. (This price was only half the cost, but Barnum shrewdly calculated it as part of his investment.)

New York was getting "Mermaid Fever."

In a day or two, an advertisement appeared prominently in the papers. It was not the usual Barnum-type ad, but it was set in a dignified and scholarly typeface rather than the customary large capitals, exclamation points, curlicues and dingbats.

The ad read:

The Mermaid, and Other Wonderful Specimens of the Animal Creation

The public are respectfully informed that, in accordance with numerous and urgent solicitations from scientific gentlemen in this city, Mr. J. Griffin, proprietor of the Mermaid, recently arrived from Pernambuco, South America, has consented to exhibit it to the public *positively for one week only!* For this purpose he has procured the spacious saloon known as Concert Hall, 404 Broadway, which will open on Monday, August 8, 1842, and will positively close on Saturday the 13th inst.

This animal was taken near the Fejee Islands, and purchased for a large sum by the present proprietor, for the Lyceum of Natural History in London, and is exhibited for this short period more for the gratification of the public than for gain. The proprietor, having been engaged for several years in various parts of the world in collecting wonderful specimens in Natural History, also has in his possession, and will at the same time submit to public inspection: THE ORNITHORHIN-CHUS, from New Holland, being the connecting link between the Seal and the Duck. THE FLYING FISH, two distinct species, one from the Gulf Stream and the other from the West Indies. This animal evidently connects the Bird with the Fish. THE PADDLE-TAIL SNAKE from South America. THE SIREN or MUD IGUANA, an intermediate animal between the Reptile and the Fish. THE PROTEUS SANGUIRUS, a subterraneous animal from a grotto in Australia—and other animals forming connecting links in the great chain of Animated Nature.

Tickets of admission 25 cents each.

It would appear that even when announcing such a highly scientific venture as Dr. Griffin's educational exhibit, Barnum was unable to prevent the style of the "Prince of Humbugs" from flowing from his pen.

The mermaid remained, as advertised, at Concert Hall for a week—where Dr. J. Griffin (Levi Lyman), surrounded by his potpourri of Natural History hocus-pocus, enlightened the large crowds upon scientific works in general, with particular emphasis on mermaids. It was then announced in the papers that the London Lyceum had at last granted Mr. P. T. Barnum's request to show it at his famous museum, provided that there be no extra charge.

On opening day, Barnum put up a huge, vibrantly colored banner in front of the museum, depicting a beautiful mermaid eighteen feet long. Upon seeing it, even Lyman balked. Such a preposterous flag had to come down, he insisted.

"But it's only to catch the public eye," Barnum protested. "Besides, it cost me seventy dollars."

"Maybe so," Lyman declared. "But nobody will believe our little dried-up specimen of fish and monkey after seeing that picture. Remember, I'm the one who has to deliver the lecture. Either the flag goes, or I go!"

Since Barnum couldn't do without Dr. Griffin, the monstrous banner came down, and stayed down.

Barnum had used the mermaid chiefly to advertise the regular business of the museum. And it worked so effectively that during the first four weeks the box-office receipts almost tripled.

P. T. confessed that he was "not proud" of the fact that such a piece of nonsense as the Fiji mermaid attracted so much more attention than did the genuine and authentic exhibits. But business, he admitted, was business—and the sharp businessman never asked a dollar where it came from.

Newspapers all over the country carried the mermaid story. When its audiences at the museum began to thin out, Barnum sent it on tour—directing the agent who went with it to advertise the curiosity as being "From Barnum's Great American Museum in New York."

8

The Mighty Midget

On a blustery November day in 1842, not quite a year after he had acquired his museum, Barnum was in Albany, New York, on business. Since the Hudson River was frozen and he would have to return to New York by train instead of boat, he decided to stop over in Bridgeport for a night with his brother, Philo, who kept the local hotel.

As the brothers sat around the blazing fire that evening, P. T. Barnum suddenly remembered something.

"Philo," he said, "I've heard tell of a remarkably small child here in town. A real dwarf. Is there any truth to it?"

"There sure is," Philo replied. "You're talking about little Charlie Stratton. He's at least five years old and not much bigger than a newborn baby."

"Does he seem all right in the head?"

"I'd say little Charlie is one of the brightest young'uns in Bridgeport," Philo assured him.

Barnum's lump of curiosity began to itch with more than its usual intensity. Could Philo get the child over to the hotel in the morning?

Barnum was nearly floored when he saw little Charles S. Stratton the next morning. The boy was only twenty-three inches tall and weighed about fifteen pounds, yet his body was perfectly formed in every respect. There was nothing of the misshapen arms, legs or torso about him that marks a dwarf. Charlie Stratton was proportioned just like any other child, although on an incredibly smaller scale.

His eyes were bright and looked out keenly and curiously from beneath his shock of light hair. His plump little cheeks, made ruddy by playing outdoors in the wintry weather, beamed with perfect health. At first he was inclined to be bashful and shy in the presence of his elders, but soon he was chatting away easily and, Barnum thought, far more intelligently than the average boy of his age.

Little Charlie's brief history, Barnum soon discovered, was a curious one. He had been a perfectly normal child at birth, weighing a few ounces more than nine pounds. At seven months, his weight had increased to fifteen pounds, just as it properly should have. Then, for no apparent reason, he simply stopped growing. We know now that such deviations from normal body development— dwarfism, giantism, extreme obesity and the like—are caused by a malfunctioning of the pituitary gland. But in those days it was all a complete mystery.

Nothing like this had ever happened before in the Stratton family. Both of Charlie's parents were normal-sized people. Charlie's two younger sisters, Frances, four, and Mary, two, were also entirely normal. At first it was difficult for the Strattons to accept their son's abnormality. But after a while they came to look upon it as just one of those things that God sometimes wills to happen—and the people of Bridgeport became so used to seeing the little boy at play with their own children that, according to most accounts, his diminutive size ceased to be a curiosity.

To Barnum, however, little Charlie was a curiosity indeed. "After seeing him and talking to him," P. T. remembered, "I at once determined to secure his services from his parents and exhibit him in public."

This was not difficult since Sherwood Stratton was a carpenter to whom every dollar came the hard way. It was like "found money" when Barnum offered to pay him $3 a week, plus traveling and living expenses for the boy and his mother. The first contract with the Strattons was for only four weeks, since—who could tell?—the lad might suddenly start growing normally again.

Now Barnum started his promotion and advertising campaign for the museum's new oddity. To begin with, a midget with such a prosaic name as Charles Stratton, from such a nearby and prosaic town as Bridgeport, Connecticut, would not attract much undue attention. Searching for a more exotic name, Barnum remembered the old fantasy of Tom Thumb, midget-pet of a legendary king. He also knew that the American public had a weakness for titles and distinguished foreigners. Furthermore, five years was not quite old enough to cause much excitement. Barnum upped his age to eleven.

And so on the museum's ads and billboards, Charles S. Stratton of Bridgeport became:

General Tom Thumb!
The Celebrated Dwarf of Eleven Years of Age!
Just Arrived From England!

Barnum spent all of the first week, working day and night, at the task of training and educating his little prodigy. He found that Charlie was an apt pupil, extremely talented for show business, unusually bright and eager to learn—and that, even at his age, he had a well-developed sense of humor and a gift for improvisation.

Before his first performance, Barnum took Tom Thumb around town to meet the most influential newspapermen. They were delighted by his charming manners and quickness of wit. The result was a flood of free publicity on the day of the General's debut.

There was a full house in the Lecture Room of the museum when Tom Thumb made his first appearance. He opened with a monologue written by Barnum that went something like:

"Good evening, ladies and gentlemen. I am only a Thumb, but a good hand at amusing you. Although a mite, I am mighty. In short, don't make much of me, for making more would be making me less. . . ." And so on for several more minutes of the funny, punny lines that P. T. was so good at writing.

Then came a few more minutes of conversation with Barnum concerning his background and his size—not very serious but punctuated with the humorous quips that little Charlie was so expert at delivering. For this part of the act, he was dressed in full military uniform.

Tom Thumb was a success on his very first appearance on Barnum's stage. For every one of his performances the Lecture Room was packed. He ordinarily did two shows a day, one in the afternoon and one in the evening. Between shows, he stood for short intervals on the "freak" stage next to the giants and the fat men.

Tom Thumb became the "hit show" that no one in town wanted to miss—the attraction about which it became fashionable to say, "And, of *course,* you've seen General Tom Thumb, Mr. Barnum's amusing little dwarf." P. T. began enlarging the act. Little Charlie appeared, appropriately costumed, as David fighting the Goliaths (two giants named Colonel Goshen and Monsieur Bihin); as a winged Cupid with his bow and sling of arrows; as Napoleon in full uniform with his hand tucked regally inside his coatfront; and as numerous other characters out of history and legend.

When the original four-week contract was up, Barnum rehired him for a year at a salary of $7 a week plus a year-end bonus—$25. The new contract provided that Barnum could show him anywhere in the United States, with both his parents accompanying him and all expenses paid.

Thereafter Tom Thumb would appear for several weeks at a time in the museum. When Barnum wished to introduce new novelties, Tom Thumb would be sent on tours of the principal cities, shepherded by Fordyce Hitchcock, one of Barnum's most trusted aides. Before long, the Mighty Midget became famous throughout the whole country.

Largely because of Tom Thumb's success, Barnum too had come to be known nationwide as America's greatest showman. Although he had made his deal for the American Museum only two years before, he now owned it lock, stock and barrel. All his debts had been paid and he had a healthy balance in the bank. The museum, now an established success, was running itself so smoothly and so profitably that P. T. felt it could be left, for extended periods at least, in the able hands of his associates.

Now Barnum again became restless. He longed once more for the excitement of the open road, for the adventures and rewards that always lay just over the horizon. Naturally his eyes turned eastward, toward the other side of the Atlantic. He had never been to Europe and he had always wanted to see a foreign country. Particularly, he wanted to find out for himself whether men and women in that part of the world were as curious—and as eager to part with their money to satisfy that curiosity—as the folks were over here. Tom Thumb, alone of all the rarities that he had shown to the public, seemed to be the ideal passport to such an adventure.

Accordingly, Barnum tore up his existing contract with Sherwood Stratton and drew up a new one for another year. It provided that Tom Thumb would receive $50 a week, and that both his parents, as well as a private tutor, would go along on the European tour with expenses paid for all. Probably to relieve Sherwood's Yankee conscience of the idea that he was living on the peculiarity of his little son, Barnum gave him the job of ticket seller.

The party sailed on January 18, 1844, aboard the *Yorkshire,* bound for Liverpool. Before leaving, Barnum had advised the newspapers in Liverpool of the impending arrival of the American wonder-dwarf, General Tom Thumb—and he had contracted with the editor of the New York *Atlas* to send back a series of columns on his European adventures. Even while he was abroad, P. T. wanted to be sure that his name appeared regularly in the New York press.

Barnum took his entourage to Europe "cold." That is, he had not tried to make advance bookings. But he had armed himself with letters of introduction to a few influential people in England, including the Honorable Edward Everett, United States Ambassador.

Even he could not foresee, he related a long time afterwards, his phenomenal triumphs. He expected at least a moderate success, but he had no idea that he would meet kings and queens and noblemen—nor that money would pour in on him in such vast quantities that it staggered the normally unstaggerable Barnum imagination.

But, ironically, the venture started off in the worst possible way, and Barnum's first reaction was that of almost abject despair.

On the evening of their arrival in England, he had his first caller, the owner of a waxworks museum. The man had heard of Tom Thumb's arrival and offered Barnum what he considered the magnificent amount of $10 a week to exhibit the General in his show. Barnum quickly showed the man the door. But it set him to worrying that dwarfs, even such an attractive one as Tom Thumb, might find little hope for success in England.

The next evening, Barnum met a distinguished-looking couple whose appearance seemed to indicate not only intelligence but wealth. They were much taken by Tom Thumb's manners and alertness and suggested that Barnum show him in Manchester, the city in which they lived. Barnum thanked them for their interest, and ventured to inquire what they thought he should ask as an admission price.

"The little General is such a curiosity," the lady suggested, "that I think you might charge as high as tuppence."

"No, no," her husband objected. "You should charge only one penny. That is the usual price for seeing giants and dwarfs."

This interchange plunged Barnum into a fit of gloom.

If this was a typical English reaction, his ambitious project would be a failure.

But in a few days his gloominess changed once more into the optimism that was Barnum's chief stock-in-trade. Some of his letters of introduction began to bring him into contact with several of Liverpool's most influential people. As a result, he rented a hall and began to show the General with something more nearly like the Barnum idea of success.

During the Liverpool engagement, the manager of the Princess Theater in London came up to see the tiny General's act. He offered Barnum a long-term contract, but Barnum was willing to exhibit Tom Thumb at the Princess for only three nights. He regarded the brief Princess engagement as only a showcase, a glorified advertisement.

The plan worked. The three-day appearance at the Princess was a smash hit. At the end of that short time Tom Thumb had become the darling of London society, the favorite topic of London conversation just as he had been the talk of New York. The Princess' manager—overwhelmed by Tom Thumb's spectacular success, and overjoyed by the box-office receipts—begged Barnum to sign for a reengagement at far higher terms. But P. T. politely refused. Everything was going his way.

Barnum took a furnished mansion on Grafton Street in London's fashionable West End, complete with butler and full household staff. He then began sending out invitations to various members of the nobility, as well as the most influential newspaper editors. Tom Thumb added to his growing luster by captivating them all.

Among the first of these visitors was Ambassador Edward Everett. He, too, fell under the little General's magic charm and promised to use his influence to arrange a personal meeting between the diminutive American General Tom Thumb and Her Majesty, Queen Victoria. This was what Barnum had been working toward. A Command Performance for the Queen would unlock every door in London for Barnum and his little gold-plated star.

During the same week, Barnum and the General received an invitation from the Baroness Rothschild, wife of the wealthiest banker in the world and the leader of London society. Arriving at the magnificent Rothschild mansion in the Baroness' carriage, the Americans were ushered up a broad flight of marble steps into a great drawing room where they met the Baroness and some two dozen other ladies and gentlemen who had been invited for the occasion.

For nearly two hours, Tom regaled them with his songs, his dances and his ready flow of wit. He impersonated various famous people, and even dared to hurl gentle, honey-coated barbs at English manners and protocol.

As Barnum was leaving, he tells us, "A well-filled purse was quietly slipped into my hand. The golden shower had begun to fall. That it was no dream was manifest from the fact that, very shortly afterwards, a visit to the mansion of Mr. Drummond, another eminent banker, came to the same golden conclusion."

Now Barnum was ready to make his move. He engaged the Egyptian Hall, in Piccadilly. And at every performance the house was jammed.

A few days after the opening, an officer of the Queen's Life Guards, wearing full dress uniform, arrived at Barnum's house with an invitation for "General Tom Thumb and his guardian, Mr. Barnum" to appear at Buckingham Palace. It was the Queen's desire, the officer said, that the General appear before her as he would before anyone else, with no special instructions as to the use of titles or the prescribed conduct in the presence of royalty. In other words, Victoria wanted Tom Thumb to be himself.

Making the most of the event, Barnum put a sign on the door of the Egyptian Hall:

"Closed this evening, General Tom Thumb being at Buckingham Palace by command of Her Majesty."

It was amazing that a boy not yet eight years old—brought up in a Connecticut country town and with the added handicap (if handicap it was) of being no larger than an infant—could so easily have become a witty, articulate and sophisticated young man overnight. Yet little Charlie Stratton somehow had that ability, and it made all the difference between being just a stunted dwarf on a "freak stage" and the perfect little man-about-town.

Dressed in court clothes—knee breeches and cutaway coats—Tom Thumb and Barnum were conducted into the presence of the Queen, her consort Prince Albert, and the court. Tom at once stepped forward, looking, Barnum said, like an animated wax doll, bowed gallantly, and said: "Good evening, ladies and gentlemen!"

The Queen was delighted—especially since the General was actually so much smaller than she had expected him to be—and, taking him by the hand, led him around the big room, speaking very informally and asking him questions about himself. To all of them Tom made whimsical answers, ad-libbing jokes and puns that kept the young Queen in a gay, lighthearted mood.

For the next hour, Tom entertained with his repertory of songs, dances and imitations, and then, after a good round of applause, the party was permitted to leave.

It was customary when leaving the presence of the Queen, to walk out backwards so that you were always facing her. Barnum, a little awed by the assembled royalty, began backing out with rather longer steps than usual, forgetting for the moment Tom Thumb's much shorter strides. But when the General saw that he was losing ground, he turned around, ran a few steps to catch up, and then solemnly turned his face toward the Queen and continued to walk out primly backwards. Since the exit hall was a long one, Tom Thumb repeated this maneuver several times, until the Queen and all her party were roaring with unroyal laughter.

On two more occasions, Barnum and the little General were invited back to the palace for Command Performances. On one such visit, the Queen requested that he sing a song and asked which one he preferred.

Without hesitating, Tom said: "Yankee Doodle."

Barnum expected the Queen and her court to be a little shocked, but the young Victoria smiled and said graciously, "That is a very pretty song, General. Please sing it."

When he met the Prince of Wales (later King Edward VII), who at that time was only three years old, Tom looked up at him and said, "The Prince is taller than I am, but I feel as big as anybody." Whereupon he strutted up and down the room, and everyone laughed and applauded this cute impertinence.

After each of Tom Thumb's appearances at Buckingham Palace, Barnum received, by uniformed Queen's Messenger, an envelope containing a handsome fee. But these fees were only a small part of Barnum's financial reward. Now that General Tom Thumb had been given the Queen's stamp of approval, so to speak, he became more than ever the rage of London. The theater was sold out, often well in advance, for every show.

It was not unusual, Barnum remembered, to see fifty or

sixty carriages, each one bearing a noble coat of arms upon its doors, lined up at the same time in front of Egyptian Hall.

In addition to his three daily appearances. Tom, with Barnum always at his side, attended three or four private parties each week, sometimes two in the same evening. And for each of these Barnum received a fee. At these parties Tom met, and was treated as a sort of pet, by such distinguished personages as the Emperor of Russia, the Kings of Belgium and Saxony, the Dukes of Buckingham, Bedford and Devonshire, Lord Robert Peel, Lord Chesterfield and many other noblemen.

When he was introduced to the Duke of Wellington, who, as the conqueror of Napoleon Bonaparte, was England's reigning hero, Tom happened to be dressed in his Napoleon costume. At the Iron Duke's approach, Tom at once assumed a pose of deep meditation.

"What are you thinking about so seriously, General?" Wellington asked.

Much to the Duke's delight, Tom promptly replied: "I was thinking, sir, about the loss of the battle of Waterloo."

One afternoon, Tom and Barnum received an invitation to call upon Victoria's aunt, the Dowager Queen Adelaide, at her Marlborough House residence. After he had sung his songs and gone through the rest of his act, the kindly old Queen Mother lifted Tom up on her lap.

"My dear little General," she said, "I see that you have no watch. Will you permit me to have a gold watch and chain made especially for you?"

For once Tom Thumb was not the wisecracking midget genius. He was a little boy again for just a moment. Tears came to his eyes as he replied, "Thank you, Ma'am. I would like that very much."

Charles S. Stratton carried the gold watch for the rest of his life.

All England seemed to succumb to Tom Thumb's charm. Toy manufacturers came out with Tom Thumb dolls. Songs were written about him, and people danced the Tom Thumb Polka and the Tom Thumb Quadrille. Albert Smith, a famous playwright of the day, wrote a play called *Hop-O-My-Thumb*—which, like Tom's name, was also based on an ancient fairy tale—and Tom played in it for an extended run at London's Lyceum Theater and throughout the provinces.

Tom Thumb played several special engagements at the Surrey Zoological Gardens. After each performance he would climb into the basket of a balloon, which was held down with ropes by about forty men. The men would maneuver the basket over the heads of the crowd, and Tom would wave to them.

One day a gust of wind caught the ground crew off guard and jerked the ropes out of the hands of nearly half of them. The others hung on desperately as their feet began to leave the ground. Fortunately, the crowd rushed to the rescue, grabbed the legs of the men, and succeeded in pulling the basket down to safety.

Barnum and many others were obviously shaken by the incident, but as Tom Thumb stepped out of the basket, he said to P. T., "I always knew, Mr. Barnum, that I was destined to rise in the world."

The year in London had been a spectacular success— and a financial bonanza. Barnum had become a rich man, and he knew that this was only the beginning. But he also knew that it would never have been possible without his mighty midget. Throughout the entire year, he had been paying the Strattons only $50 a week as specified in their contract. The rest of the immense income had gone into Barnum's pocket.

But now that the English venture, which had started out as a speculation, had turned into a solid-gold success, Barnum determined that Tom Thumb should get his rightful share. On January 1, 1845, he drew up a new contract with the Strattons. It was a life-time agreement, and by its terms Tom Thumb and P. T. Barnum would split all profits from his exhibitions fifty-fifty. As a result, before his career was over, Tom Thumb had become a millionaire—and his father, the former carpenter, was financially independent for life.

9

The Long Road Home to Bridgeport

ALTHOUGH, even after a year and a half, London couldn't seem to get enough of Tom Thumb, Barnum decided that it was time to leave England and show his little General to some of the rest of Europe. A preliminary visit to Paris convinced him that Tom Thumb's fame had preceded him and that France was eager to see him in person.

On the day after Barnum and Tom Thumb arrived in Paris, they received an invitation from King Louis Philippe to appear at the Tuileries Palace on the following Sunday evening to give a Command Performance. Upon their arrival they were ushered into the grand salon of the palace where they were greeted with unusual informality by the King, the Queen, and members of the court.

The King was especially taken by the self-assurance of the little General, and the two were soon chatting about the wonders of America. As a young prince in exile, Louis

Philippe had spent several years wandering around the United States, and he confessed to Tom that he had once actually slept in an Indian's wigwam.

Finally Tom Thumb went into his regular act—singing, dancing, doing impersonations, joking—and he made, if possible, an even greater hit with the French King than he had with Queen Victoria. At the conclusion of Tom's performance, the King presented him with a large brooch of emeralds and diamonds, which was described by the court chronicler as being "so big that the General could have used it as a dress sword." In addition, Tom was plied with so many other expensive gifts that when he went back to his hotel his arms were loaded with a small fortune in jewelry.

Encouraged by the warmth and good-fellowship of the King's reception, Barnum asked a royal favor. The annual Longchamps holiday was coming soon, and Barnum asked if Tom Thumb's carriage could be permitted in the royal section of the grand parade up the Champs Elysées and into the Bois de Boulogne. He explained that the General's carriage was so small, and the ponies that pulled it so tiny, that it might be damaged if it was driven in any other part of the procession.

Tom Thumb's miniature carriage had been built in London to Barnum's order. The coach, only eleven inches long and twenty inches high, was elaborately decorated and furnished inside and out. The Shetland ponies that drew the carriage were equally fantastic. A perfectly matched four-in-hand, they were just thirty-four inches high, and their long tails swept the pavement behind them.

"Call the Prefect of Police tomorrow afternoon," the King replied at once, "and you will find a permit ready for you."

Tom Thumb's equipage drew more enthusiastic attention than did that of Louis Philippe. And the throngs that lined the sidewalks to watch the parade filled the warm spring air of Paris with shouts of *"Vive le Tom Pouce!"*

As Barnum put it: "What in London is only excitement, in Paris becomes furore." The city was making an idol of "Tom Pouce." Seats at all afternoon and evening performances were sold out at premium prices as much as two months in advance. The papers and magazines were full of his pictures. Statuettes of the little General done in sugar and chocolate appeared in dozens of shop windows. Songs were written about him. Well-known painters vied with each other to do his portrait.

As he had in England, Tom appeared in a play, *Petit Poucet,* written especially for him. He was elected a member of the exclusive French Dramatic Society. He was in constant demand to appear at private parties and entertainments. Barnum "complained" that the money came in so fast, and in such huge amounts, that he had to hire a cab to carry it to the bank.

Because of the demands of other cities, Barnum reluctantly closed the stand in Paris and took Tom Thumb on an extended tour of the French provinces—to Orléans, Nantes, Brest, Bordeaux, Toulouse, Montpellier, Marseilles and almost all the other principal cities of France. Then crossing the Belgian border near Lille, the tour proceeded to Brussels.

The Belgian border guards were so impressed by Tom Thumb's grand entourage that they politely inquired what rank he held in his own country.

"He is Prince Charles Stratton, of the Dukedom of

Bridgeport, in the Kingdom of Connecticut!" Barnum told them solemnly.

In awe the guards removed their hats and passed the whole party—costumes, scenery, props, trophies, coach-and-four—through customs duty-free.

In England, Barnum had had several thousand medals made up which he sold as souvenirs at Tom Thumb's shows. They had Tom's likeness on the obverse and those of Queen Victoria and Prince Albert on the reverse. Grandly, Barnum dug into the handiest crate of medals and decorated the customs officials.

From a tour of Belgium—which included a Command Performance before King Leopold and his Queen—Barnum took the show back to England, Scotland and Ireland for another round of appearances in Great Britain. At last, after slightly more than three years abroad, Barnum closed his triumphant European tour in Dublin and the troupe set sail for New York.

Charlie Stratton felt that he needed a vacation back home in Bridgeport, for he had been away from home for nearly five years, working steadily. Barnum agreed. But first, in order to capitalize promptly on his European reputation—all details of which had been reported regularly by P. T. in his dispatches for the *Atlas*—it was decided that he should appear for a month at the old stand in the American Museum. All attendance records were smashed.

Then back to Bridgeport went Charlie—now by all odds the best-known boy in the world.

Upon his arrival, he put on his show for a few days at a Bridgeport auditorium so that everyone in town could see his act. The receipts went to the Bridgeport Charitable Society. Then he retired to his father's home for a month of relaxing and doing nothing except to stroll around town and chat with old friends when he met them on the street. No longer did he play with the other boys his age. Although he hadn't increased an inch in height since he had left home, his stature had grown tremendously insofar as his mind, his personality and his outlook upon life were concerned. Charlie Stratton at ten was no longer a little boy. He was a tiny man.

"We never thought of little Charlie as much of a curiosity when he lived among us," one prominent citizen said. "But now that he has been 'Barnumized' he is a rare little gentleman."

And indeed he was. Barnum had provided Tom Thumb with the best of tutors, and his quick mind had made the most of his opportunities for learning. He spoke a little French as well as impeccable English. Since he had rubbed shoulders on a personal basis with European royalty, he was not awed by his elders—with the possible exception of P. T. Barnum, who was his idol.

"The General left America three years before, a diffident, uncultivated little boy," Barnum wrote. "He came back an educated, accomplished little man. He had seen much and profited much. He went abroad poor, and he came home rich."

Since half of his ten years had been spent in show business, the magic of stage center was in little Charlie Stratton's blood. A month of loafing around Bridgeport was all that his restless, and strangely adult, temperament could take. He couldn't wait to get back into the spotlight. General Tom Thumb was the smallest—yet one of the biggest—hams that ever lived.

Barnum agreed to accompany him for the first year of a protracted tour of the United States. The road-showing

began in April, 1847, in Washington, D.C., where the first
item on the schedule was an invitation to have dinner
with President James K. Polk. From there it covered vir-
tually all the Atlantic Coast states, the South, Cuba and the
Midwest.

At Pittsburgh, in May, 1848, Barnum left the tour to
return to his business affairs in New York. Thereafter,
throughout most of the thirty years of the Barnum-Stratton
association as equal partners, a trusted Barnum agent
traveled with the Tom Thumb company as general manager and advance man. The one exception was ten years
later, when Barnum and the General made a triumphant
return tour of Europe.

In 1862 Tom Thumb, now twenty-four years old, had
grown to thirty-three inches in height and weighed fifty
pounds. He was a wealthy man, with a country estate outside Bridgeport, a stable of fine, blooded horses, and a
large yacht which he sailed on Long Island Sound. The
demand for his appearance, all over the United States
as well as in England, France and Germany, was as great
as ever. But now he spent longer intervals between tours
at home, since sailing—next to show business—was the
prime interest of his life.

In 1862 P. T. Barnum heard of a midget girl, Lavinia
Warren, who lived in Middleboro, Massachusetts. She was
twenty years old, thirty-two inches tall, and weighed twenty-
nine pounds. She was intelligent and well-educated—so
much so that, in spite of her diminutive size, she had been
a third-grade teacher in the Middleboro school. In addition
to her mental attributes, she had a perfectly formed feminine body and a face like a lovely doll.

Barnum hurried off at once to Middleboro and put her

under contract at a handsome salary. Wearing expensive clothes and jewelry, Lavinia became the "star" of the museum show.

One day that autumn, Charlie Stratton, then between tours, dropped in at the museum to have lunch with Barnum. When he saw Lavinia he was stricken. After Barnum had made the proper introductions and the two little people had chatted briefly, Charlie asked his mentor if he could see him privately, and at once, in his office.

"Mr. Barnum," he said, "I am in love. That is the most beautiful and charming little lady I have seen in my life, and I believe that she was created for the sole purpose of being my wife. You and I are old friends. Will you put in a good word for me?"

"Well, General," Barnum grinned, amused and a little amazed at his protégé's sudden ardor, "I'm all for you. But you'll have to do your own courting. And," he cautioned, "I'd advise you not to go too fast. Miss Warren is a very sensitive girl."

For the next several weeks Tom Thumb was constantly underfoot at the museum, spending every moment with Lavinia that he could possibly find an excuse for. Finally, he persuaded Barnum to invite her to his Connecticut home for a weekend.

"And ask me for the weekend at your house too, sir," Tom added. "I intend to pop the question."

And pop it he did. For a verbatim account of the actual proposal we are indebted to two curious young ladies who were also guests of the Barnums. When Tom and Lavinia went by themselves into a sitting room after dinner on the first evening for a game of backgammon, the nosy little teenagers seated themselves on the stairs in a darkened hallway just outside the door. From this vantage point they heard easily all that was said. Their version of the "question popping" scene—with which both Tom and Lavinia good-naturedly agreed after the story was told and all was forgiven—went something like this:

The General soon declared that he was hopelessly beaten at backgammon. Then he remarked, "I understand you are going to Europe soon."

"Yes, Mr. Barnum intends to take me over in a couple of months."

"I wish I was going too. I have spent six years abroad and I could explain all the different countries to you." Tom paused a second, as if struck by a sudden thought. "Maybe I'll ask Mr. Barnum to take me along."

"I thought you said the other day that you had all the money you needed and were tired of traveling," Miss Warren remarked.

"That," Tom said, "depends upon my company while traveling."

"You might not find my company very agreeable."

"I would be glad to risk it."

"Then why don't you speak to Mr. Barnum?" Lavinia suggested.

"Would you really like to have me go?"

"Of course I would."

Now was the time! The little General leaned closer to her chair and put his arm around her tiny waist.

"Don't you think it would be pleasanter if we went as man and wife?"

At this point, according to the listeners, Lavinia spoke the classic line: "But this is so sudden!"

"Not sudden at all!" Tom said firmly. "The first moment I saw you I knew that you were meant to be my wife."

Lavinia hesitated for the required instant or two, then

she said softly, "I think I love you enough to say yes."

Naturally, the engagement between the two most famous little people in New York was announced with more than the customary Barnum fanfare. Tom Thumb appeared with Lavinia at the museum, and people literally fought for tickets to get in to see them together.

Barnum had promised himself to give the little couple the finest wedding that was to be had, and the date was set. But the museum crowds got bigger all the time, so much so that Barnum offered them a flat $15,000 if they would postpone the ceremony for a month and stay on for the extra time at the museum.

"Not for fifty thousand!" the General declared firmly.

Lavinia threw her arms around his neck. "Good for you, Charlie!" she exclaimed. "Only you should have said *not for a hundred thousand!*"

Although he knew that he could gross $25,000 or more if he staged the wedding at the museum and charged admission, Barnum put the idea out of his mind. After all, he decided, there were limits beyond which even the world's greatest showman could not, in good taste, go.

The ceremony took place on February 10, 1863, in New York's Grace Church. Admission was by invitation only, and the church was packed with prominent people—the Governors of several states, members of Congress, Army generals, distinguished politicians, and editors of the leading newspapers and magazines.

Barnum was besieged by people who wanted to buy invitations—for as much as $60 apiece. "But," he remembered proudly, "not a single ticket was sold."

The first stop on their wedding trip was Washington, where Abraham Lincoln took time out from the anguish of the Civil War to invite them to the White House. (President and Mrs. Lincoln, by the way, had sent them a wedding present.)

Addressing him as General, Lincoln asked Tom if he had any suggestions about the conduct of the war.

"Mr. President," Tom replied, "my friend Barnum could settle the whole thing in a month."

Charles and Lavinia Stratton had twenty years of happy marriage. Although they had originally intended to retire to Tom Thumb's estate in Bridgeport, the lure of the crowds was too much for them. Together they made a number of exhibition tours through the United States and Europe.

Pictures taken in his later years show that Tom Thumb became prosperously portly, sported a handlebar moustache, and gradually grew to be three feet, four inches tall.

Charles Stratton died of apoplexy in 1883, at the age of forty-five, and the newspapers reported that more than ten thousand people went to Bridgeport for his funeral. His grave was marked by a tall marble shaft, on top of which stood a life-sized statue of himself. Lavinia lived until 1919, and was buried next to her husband. Her tiny headstone bore only two words: "His Wife."

10
The Swedish Nightingale

In something less than six years Barnum had come to be generally acknowledged as the most successful showman in the world—a man of wealth, an international celebrity, an intimate of kings and queens and presidents.

Was it luck? Barnum said absolutely not! He said that he didn't believe in mere luck, that his success had been founded on good planning and hard work. Those qualities, along with a goodly share of pure luck, were a part of it to be sure. But Barnum's real talent lay in a sort of sixth sense that is given to few men: the indefinable ability to see and feel what lesser men are incapable of seeing or feeling—to give his boundless imagination an uninhibited rein—to know a good hunch from a bad one, and then to back it with every chip in his stack.

In 1848 Barnum was sitting on top of the world. His bank account was bulging. The American Museum, as well as his half interest in Tom Thumb's tours, provided him with a princely income. He had a staff of trusted associates who were capable of managing his day-to-day business affairs.

Like many another young man of thirty-eight who has clawed his way up from the bottom to the top in a comparatively short time—and especially one who never in all his life enjoyed the luxury of a vacation—Barnum's thoughts turned to semiretirement.

His country estate in Fairfield, Connecticut, which had been two years in the building, was ready for him to move into. At long last he and his family could live in comfortable ease. He could go to New York via the New Haven Railroad a day or two each week to make sure that all was going well at Broadway and Ann Street. For the rest of the time he could take it easy as a country squire.

Barnum being Barnum, his Fairfield home was enough to knock a beholder's eye out. It outdid almost any oddity for which he had ever charged admission. Indeed, P. T. admitted that he wanted his country place "to be unique for, with an eye to business, I thought that a pile of buildings of a novel order might indirectly serve as an advertisement for my Museum."

"Unique" was the mildest possible word he could have used to describe it. Standing on seventeen acres that overlooked Long Island Sound, the mansion by almost any standard was an architectural monstrosity.

In the resort town of Brighton, England, Barnum's eye for the bizarre had been caught by the Oriental Pavilion erected by King George IV, in the early 1800's, as a seaside residence. He was so fascinated by its off-beat design that he determined to use it as a model for his own home, and immediately engaged a London architect to duplicate the Pavilion's plans. On a brief trip to New York during Tom Thumb's run in England, he hired an architect and builder to adapt the plans to fit his Connecticut property. He admonished them to "spare neither time nor expense in erecting a comfortable, convenient and tasteful residence."

When it was finished, the house looked like something out of the Arabian Nights. One hundred and twenty-four feet wide, it was topped by a huge, ornately decorated, onion-shaped, Byzantine-type dome that towered nearly one hundred feet into the air. The central dome, in turn, was surrounded by a number of smaller domes, spires, turrets, and minarets—the whole presenting an effect not unlike, in miniature, St. Basil's Cathedral in Moscow.

Below the roofline, the two and a half stories of the house proper became abruptly Spanish-Moroccan in style. It was faced all around by dozens of arched porticos resplendent with intricate filigree and scrollwork—somewhat vaguely reminiscent of the Alhambra at Granada.

The inside of the house was dominated by a great hallway that led off to dozens of rooms—and by a wide marble stairway that rose to the floors above. The hall and the stairway were lined with paintings, statues, tapestries and other works of art that came from all over the world. Each room was adorned with furniture of a different design and period—tailor-made to Barnum's specifications.

The grounds that surrounded the mansion were parklike in their perfection. Shade trees and complete orchards, all full-grown, were transplanted as decoration. A large fountain gushed before the main entrance. The stables and other outbuildings duplicated the design of the main house. And the final touch, a rarity for its time, was a complete waterworks that supplied indoor plumbing.

Barnum called the estate "Iranistan"—meaning, in some

tongue east of Suez, "Oriental Villa." He boasted that it was the "only specimen of Oriental architecture" in America. Which was probably just as well.

The Barnum family moved in in November, 1848, and nearly a thousand invited guests—New York celebrities and Connecticut neighbors alike—came to the housewarming.

For a little more than a year, Barnum was happy in his new role as a rural landowner and family man. He enjoyed riding around in his carriage and passing the time of day with his neighbors. By virtue of the fact that he had bought an extra hundred acres of farmland and hired a man to manage it, he was elected President of the Fairfield County Agricultural Society. For obvious reasons, he was at once drafted as chairman of the annual County Fair committee. In this capacity, he pepped up admission sales by introducing such new attractions as plowing contests and work-team hauling competitions.

Then, as now, county fairs were happy hunting grounds for pickpockets. Some of the more imaginative of these gentlemen went so far as to tack up signs that read "Beware of Pickpockets." Seeing such a sign, the cautious visitor would instinctively pat the pocket that held his wallet to make sure it was still safe, thus revealing the exact location of his "poke."

On one occasion a pickpocket was arrested, admitted his guilt, and was bound for trial. At Barnum's request, the sheriff agreed to exhibit him, handcuffed, at the Fair. Shrewdly, P. T. kept this attraction on ice, so to speak, until the final day of the Fair, when admissions were expected to be light. As a result, closing day broke all attendance records, crowds of people coming back for a second time in order to get a look at a real-life—and safely trussed-up—"dip."

It was inevitable that the peace and quietude of pastoral life would soon begin to pall on the great P. T. His free-wheeling spirit once more became restless.

His reputation as America's number-one showman had been built on freaks and fakes. Even Tom Thumb—although he possessed a genuine talent for entertaining and a personality that entranced kings, queens and commoners alike—was basically an aberration of nature. But Barnum wanted something more. He wanted to cap his career with one great theatrical triumph.

His first try was big thinking at its biggest—"an extraordinary exhibition," as he put it, "that would excite universal attention and commendation in America and abroad."

This was a "Congress of Nations," representative of all humanity the world over. He proposed to procure a man and a woman—the most physically perfect specimen that could be found—"from every accessible group of people, civilized and barbarous, on the face of the globe."

This undertaking turned out to be just a little *too* big, even for P. T. Barnum. But while he was working at it, he was suddenly bowled over one day with an even bigger idea—a proposition that would be much easier to handle, if indeed it could be accomplished at all.

He, Phineas T. Barnum, would bring the great Jenny Lind to America under his own personal management! Jenny Lind, the golden-voiced "Swedish Nightingale"! The sweetest singer the world had ever known! The simple peasant girl who, by the magic of her music, had all Europe at her feet!

"As I recall it now," Barnum later wrote, "I almost tremble at the temerity of the attempt. That I am proud of it

I freely confess. It placed me before the world in an entirely new light."

Yes! Jenny Lind would make him the *new* Barnum that he had dreamed of being—a maestro, a true impresario, a patron of culture and the arts!

He had never heard Jenny Lind sing, but that didn't matter. Her glorious European reputation was all he needed. Barnum calculated that a Jenny Lind tour of the United States, properly ballyhooed in advance and astutely managed, should bring him a fortune. But if it should somehow turn out to be a financial turkey, he decided that he was willing to lose up to $50,000 "for the distinction of bringing to this country, at the zenith of her life and celebrity, the greatest musical wonder of the world."

Jenny Lind and company arrived in New York on the steamship *Atlantic* on August 21, 1850. Barnum boarded the ship at Staten Island with the U. S. Health Department officer, and met his songbird for the first time.

When the ship pulled in to its berth at a Canal Street wharf, the surrounding docks, piers and streets were covered by a living carpet of cheering people all eager to catch a sight of the fabulous girl with the golden voice. In the pushing and shoving, one man fell into the water, alarming Jenny but amusing Barnum, who told her that the man was simply overwhelmed by her loveliness.

Barnum escorted his star down the gangplank, beneath a bower of flag-decorated green trees, and under two immense floral archways, one spelling out: "Welcome, Jenny Lind!" and the other "Welcome to America!"

Handing Jenny into a waiting carriage, Barnum directed the driver to the Irving House. Barnum himself sat on top beside the driver, waving and tipping his hat to the thousands of spectators who lined the streets.

Such enthusiasm for a visiting celebrity had rarely if ever been seen in New York. Within a few minutes, some 20,000 people had congregated around the Broadway entrance to the hotel, yelling for the great Jenny to appear on the balcony. The New York Musical Society's 200-piece band, accompanied by 300 uniformed firemen all carrying brightly lit torches, arrived as twilight fell and began a serenade. Barnum led Jenny out onto a balcony, and the acclaim grew even more tumultuous.

The first concert was scheduled for September 11, which gave Barnum almost another month for Jenny Lind promotion. Songs and new dances were named for her; Jenny Lind dresses appeared in the shops, along with Jenny Lind hats, Jenny Lind shawls, Jenny Lind robes, all sorts of Jenny Lind furniture from pianos to tea tables—to say nothing of the merchant ship, the brand of whiskey, and the racehorse that were each christened "Jenny Lind." Her rooms were continually crowded with distinguished visitors, the elite of New York politics and society. Whenever Barnum took her out for a sightseeing tour of the city, her carriage was literally mobbed by admirers.

Barnum hired Castle Garden, the largest auditorium in the city for Jenny's first performance and decided to sell the tickets for her premier performance at auction. Then he went to his old friend John Genin, who owned a hat store across the street from the museum, and advised him to buy the first ticket offered regardless of the cost. The man who bought ticket number one, Barnum assured him, would get his picture in every paper in the country and his fortune would be made.

The auction took place on Saturday, and although the

management of the Garden charged everyone a shilling (about 12½ cents) to get in, about 3,000 people showed up.

Bidding for the first ticket went up and up and up, but John Genin hung on until it was finally his for $225. All told, $17,864 worth of tickets were sold for that single performance.

Barnum's hunch about Genin proved correct. His name became famous all over America, and soon men were paying premium prices for a hat with the Genin label. As Barnum predicted, the $225 ticket made him a fortune.

The first Lind concert was brought off with typical Barnum flair. The entire interior of Castle Garden had been divided into four sections, each lighted and decorated in a different color. By means of colored tickets, customers were quickly directed to their seats by the hundreds of ushers who wore colored rosettes and carried canes wrapped with colored ribbons. Altogether, an audience of 5,000 people—by far the largest crowd to which Jenny Lind had ever sung—was jammed rafter-high in the Garden.

"The reception of Jenny Lind," Barnum wrote, "in point of enthusiasm, was probably never before equaled in the world. As she approached the footlights, the entire audience rose to their feet and welcomed her with a storm of thunderous applause and a mighty sea of waving handkerchiefs."

When the cheering had subsided, and Jenny began at last to sing, the great crowd quieted so as not to miss a single note. But at the end of her first number, the cheering and applause was ear-splitting. At the conclusion of the program, she was called back time after time for curtain calls.

Then came shouts of "Barnum! Barnum!" and P. T.,

hand in hand with his prima donna, came forward and took a modest bow.

In Jenny Lind, Barnum had the biggest attraction that had ever appeared on the American stage. Her triumph, and Barnum's, had been complete! So began the nine months of mostly pleasant association between Barnum and his Swedish Nightingale that was to earn nearly $177,000 for Jenny and more than half a million for Barnum. Altogether, under Barnum's management, Jenny gave ninety-five concerts—thirty-five in New York and others in cities from Boston to New Orleans and Havana, and as far west as St. Louis. Virtually all of them matched the tremendous reception that she had received on her first night in Castle Garden.

For the most part the tour was fun for Jenny, who had known very little about touring, even during her years of supreme success on the Continent. She liked the big, hearty, fun-loving Barnum, and even came to delight in some of the tricks that P. T. played on the crowds of admirers that followed her wherever she went.

Barnum always saw to it that great multitudes were on hand to greet Jenny upon her arrival at every city on the itinerary. But the Nightingale preferred to arrive quietly and without fanfare, since the task of making her way through the crowds was a severe strain on her nerves. She could never understand how thousands of admirers could have gathered together to greet her. Barnum, of course, never let her know it was part of his scheme for making sure that the theaters were always packed for her concerts. He did, however, go out of his way whenever he could to make things easier for her.

When Jenny, Barnum and company arrived in Philadelphia from New York, they literally had to fight their way through the cheering crowd, which then followed their carriages to Jones' Hotel. There, thousands of people congregated outside and shouted for Jenny to appear on the balcony. The poor girl was suffering from a severe headache, and had gone to bed, with her maid applying cold cloths to her forehead. Barnum went to the window and, quieting the shouts, attempted to explain the situation. He assured them that there would be seats for all at the concert that night, and asked them *please* to show some consideration for the great diva's feelings. But they yelled him down, and shouted that they would leave when—and not until—Jenny Lind came out to greet them.

Barnum finally lifted both arms into the air for silence. If they would be patient for just one more minute or two, he said, he would produce Jenny Lind for them.

Inside, he placed Jenny's bonnet and shawl on her traveling companion, Miss Ahmansen, and led her out onto the balcony. As the mob roared, Miss Ahmansen donned her prettiest smile, waved gaily, took several bows, and promised them that she would sing as she had never sung before—especially for them—when they came to hear her that evening at the concert hall.

Later in the tour, as they came in to New Orleans aboard the steamer *Falcon,* the wharf was swarming with well-wishers, all waving flags and banners and shouting "Welcome Jenny!"

Standing on the deck, Jenny clutched P. T.'s arm in despair. "Oh dear! Mr. Barnum," she whispered. "How can I ever get through all those people?"

"Leave it to me," Barnum assured her. "Wait right here for ten minutes, and there won't be any crowd left."

Caroline, Barnum's oldest daughter, had come along on this trip and now Barnum held out his arm to her. "Cover your face with your veil," he instructed her, "as if you were displaying great modesty, and come along with me."

At that point, one of Barnum's crew appeared at the head of the gangway and began to shout: "Stand back there! Make way for Mr. Barnum and Miss Lind! No crowding or jostling, please! You will all have a chance to see them!"

Whereupon Barnum and Caroline stepped down to the wharf and started for the waiting carriage.

"Don't crowd her, if you please, gentlemen!" Barnum kept repeating, as the two finally fought their way to the carriage and drove off to the hotel, the cheering mob following at their heels.

In a moment or so the wharf was empty, and Jenny and Miss Ahmansen strolled to the second carriage. Once safely inside the hotel, Jenny appeared on the balcony of her room, as had become her custom, and waved a happy greeting to the thousands of her admirers.

From New Orleans the Lind Company made its way up the Mississippi and Ohio rivers for concerts in the leading river cities. At the Cincinnati wharf, a crowd was waiting that was even larger, louder and more enthusiastic than had been the one at New Orleans. Since the New Orleans debarkation ruse had been printed in all the Cincinnati paper as a part of Barnum's publicity deluge, he knew that in order to get Jenny through the mob quietly he would have to pull something different out of the hat.

When the gangplank was secured to the wharf, P. T. led the way off the boat with a smiling Jenny Lind demurely holding his arm. As they took the first step, a voice from the deck—one of the passengers, or so everyone assumed— gave out with a loud guffaw and shouted: "It's no go, Mr. Barnum! You can't pass your daughter off for Jenny Lind this time!"

At this the crowd began good-naturedly to laugh and catcall:

"That's right, Barnum, you old faker!"

"You may fool the people in New Orleans, but you can't put it over on us Buckeyes!"

"We're waiting right here till you trot out the *real* Jenny Lind!"

Barnum threw up his hands in mock defeat and joined the general merriment.

"All right, boys," he admitted. "You're too slick for me. Just stick around a minute. She'll be along in two shakes."

And while the crowd waited, eyes glued to the deck for a glimpse of the *real* Jenny, Barnum and his Nightingale proceeded peacefully and quietly to their hotel.

Caroline Barnum was again with the company when it arrived in Baltimore. On the first Sunday morning of their stay in town, Jenny Lind was resting after her concert of the night before—but the Barnums, regular churchgoers, attended services with a friend who lived in the city. The friend was a member of the choir, and invited Caroline to come up to the choir loft with her and join the singing.

Meanwhile, the congregation had recognized Barnum and assumed that the beautiful young woman with him was Jenny Lind. There was a great gasp of astonishment when the ladies left Barnum's side and proceeded to join the other members of the choir.

The incomparable Jenny Lind was going to sing in their choir! The hum of excitement that filled the church fell to a dead hush as Caroline rose with the rest of the group for the singing of the opening hymn.

Now, Caroline Barnum possessed a fair, country-choir soprano, but she was not quite a "Connecticut Nightingale." Yet not a note was lost on the openmouthed congregation.

When the hymn was over and the choir had reseated itself, Barnum heard loud whispers of: "What an exquisite singer!" "Such a heavenly voice!" "I never heard the like before!"

At the end of the service, the church aisle was jammed by a polite but nonetheless curious congregation who wanted a closer look at the fabulous singer whose magic voice had been such a miraculous extra-added attraction to a usually humdrum Sunday morning. Caroline had no idea what all the fuss had been about until her father gleefully explained it on the walk home.

Only once in the long and prosperous tour did Barnum and his popular star encounter hostility. It was in Havana, where P. T. least expected it.

The trouble arose because the Habaneros resented the prices that Barnum had posted for the concerts—prices about double the amount they normally paid for seats in the Tacon Opera House. But Barnum had contracted to pay the Opera House $1,000 a night, and he had no intention of losing money. For once even the newspapers were anti-Barnum, one of them calling him a "Yankee pirate" who cared nothing for art, but "only for golden doubloons."

In spite of the city's general resentment, the Opera House was filled for Jenny's first concert. At her appearance, there was a light clatter of applause, but this was instantly drowned out by a thunderous wave of hisses. Nothing like this had ever happened to her before, and for a moment Jenny was stunned. Then, realizing at last what she was in for, her eyes flashed defiance. Most of the New York papers followed the Jenny Lind tour, and the Havana correspondent of the New York *Tribune* described the scene that ensued in these words:

She stood there, perfectly calm and beautiful, the music began, and then followed such heavenly strains as I verily believe mortal never breathed except Jenny Lind, and mortal never heard except from her lips. Some of the oldest Castilians kept a frown upon their brow and a curling sneer upon their lip; their ladies, however, and most of the audience began to look surprised. The gushing melody flowed on increasing in beauty and glory. The torrent flowed deeper and faster, the lark flew higher and higher, the melody grew richer and grander. Bye and bye, as the rich notes came dashing in rivers upon our enraptured ears, one poor critic involuntarily whispered *"brava."* This outbursting of the soul was instantly hissed down. The streams of harmony rolled on till, at the close, it made a clean sweep of every obstacle and carried all before it. Not a vestige of opposition remained, but such a tremendous shout of applause went up as I never before heard.

Trembling slowly bowing her head, Jenny Lind withdrew. The roar and applause of victory increased. *"Encore!" "Encore!" "Encore!"* came from every lip. She again appeared and curtsying low, again withdrew; but again and again and again did they call her, and at every appearance the thunder of applause rang louder and louder.

Barnum admitted that he was weeping for joy when he rushed from his private box and reached the stage just as Jenny was withdrawing from her fifth encore.

"God bless you, Jenny!" he said. "You have settled them!"

Jenny threw her arms around his neck, tears in her eyes—and Barnum declared that she had never looked so beautiful as on that all-conquering evening.

Under the pleasant surface, Barnum had begun to have trouble with his golden songbird—thanks mainly to Jenny's circle of self-appointed advisers, and in part to her own naivete and inexperience in matters of practical business.

P. T. was well aware that the immense financial success of the American tour would be sure to create much envy—and eventually malice toward him—on the part of these advisers and hangers-on. Chief among them was the male secretary that she had brought with her from Europe. Almost from the beginning, Barnum discovered, he had been covertly planning to take over as her business manager. To prepare her mind for the eventual success of his scheme, this shrewd young man continually dinned into Jenny's ears the idea that Barnum was reaping a fortune from her genius; that his publicity campaign for her concerts was more fitting for a freak like the Fiji Mermaid; that, after all, she should remember that he had made his reputation by exhibiting a midget; and that she could make far more money by ridding herself of Barnum and conducting her concerts on her own.

The matter came to a head one day when the secretary approached Barnum and announced that Miss Lind wished to cancel her contract, but, not wishing to leave Mr. Barnum out in the cold completely, she would be willing to pay him $1,000 per concert as her producer.

P. T.'s answer was an indignant refusal.

Then what would Mr. Barnum charge?

"One million dollars each," he said flatly, "and not one cent less. Remember, I hired Miss Lind in the first place, and not she me."

This set the secretary back on his heels, and Barnum heard no more about the matter for a while. But all the undercover plotting and scheming—the "wheels within wheels" as he called it—were increasingly getting on his nerves. He finally found himself hoping that he could wash his hands of the whole thing. Jenny at last resolved the difficulty by informing him, in writing, that she wished to conclude their business arrangement at his earliest convenience.

But with Barnum gone, the magic was gone. In the managerial hands of her new "advisers," box-office receipts rapidly declined, and the Jenny Lind hold upon American audiences dwindled and all but vanished.

P. T. saw her a few times afterward, and always found her most harassed and unhappy. "People cheat me and swindle me very much," she told him.

Not long afterwards she retired to Europe, where she lived out most of the rest of her life in comfortable seclusion.

11
The Congress of Freaks and Fakes

P. T. BARNUM's brief excursion into the lofty realm of the arts was good for his ego as well as his bank account. He had proved to himself, and to the public, that he could sell culture as well as curiosities. But he always felt much more at home as an uninhibited pitchman than ever he did behind the scenes of a concert stage.

And it was as a freewheeling showman, not as an impresario, that Barnum found his place in American history and folklore.

P. T. boasted that during his career he had exhibited more than a million "curiosities and educational features." This was probably no exaggeration, since the roster of Barnumiana ran all the way from run-of-the-mill fare like Indian war bonnets and "genuine South American anteaters" to such fabulous freaks as the Siamese Twins and such outlandish fakes as "Colonel Frémont's Nondescript."

While touring with General Tom Thumb in 1848, Barnum had chanced upon a small horse in Ohio that was without doubt the most unusual equine ever foaled. Its entire body, head, legs and all, was covered with fine, tightly curling, camel-colored wool. It had no mane, and its tail was as devoid of hair as a rat's. Barnum bought the creature, had it shipped to Bridgeport, and there kept carefully under wraps until some proper use could be found for it.

The occasion was not long in coming. A few months later the New York papers were full of a story about Colonel John Charles Frémont, the soldier-turned explorer, who had recently been cashiered from the Army for insubordination but who was still colorful and popular. It seemed that the Colonel, while attempting to find a new passageway through the Rocky Mountains, had been lost in a blizzard along with his entire expedition. The people mourned the passing of an intrepid hero, but rejoiced when, a week later, dispatches from the Far West announced that Frémont and most of his men had made their way safely into New Mexico.

Hard on the heels of the news about Frémont's lucky escape came an even more exciting dispatch (apparently from the same legitimate sources) to the effect that, while making their way out of the mountains, the Colonel's men had been fortunate enough to capture a most unusual "nondescript" animal—somewhat resembling a horse, but covered with a thick coat of wool—the likes of which had never been seen on earth before. The dispatch went on to say that Colonel Frémont was sending this extraordinary beast as a gift to the U. S. Army Quartermaster General.

The astounding story had scarcely run its course on the front pages before a follow-up appeared saying that the now-famous "woolly horse" was being shipped to London for examination by England's leading scientists— but that, by popular demand, it would be exhibited for a few days to the New York public en route.

Meanwhile Barnum bundled up his Ohio horse in thick blankets and leggings, so that nothing could be seen of it except eyes and hoofs, and shipped it to a stable in the rear of the Museum.

A day or so later, an advertisement appeared in all the New York papers:

> COL. FRÉMONT'S NONDESCRIPT OR WOOLLY HORSE will be exhibited for a few days only at the corner of Broadway and Reade Street, previous to its departure for London. Nature seems to have exerted all her ingenuity in the production of this astounding animal. It is extremely complex—being part Elephant, Deer, Horse, Buffalo, Camel, and Sheep, and easily bounds twelve or fifteen feet high. Naturalists and the oldest trappers assured Col. Frémont that it was never known previous to his discovery. Admittance 25 cents; children half price.

Above the doorway of the building in which the horse was stabled ran a huge, full-color painting which depicted Frémont and his fellow explorers chasing the fleeing Nondescript, which was bounding away in 12-and 15-foot leaps.

The public eagerly lined up on opening day to lay down their quarters. After a successful showing in New York and several nearby cities, Barnum sent his horse to Washington, under the management of an agent, "to see if the wool could be pulled over the eyes of the politicians."

For several days the show was a hit. Then crusty old Thomas Hart Benton, the powerful senator from Missouri and Frémont's father-in-law, sued Barnum's agent for fraud. He claimed that if any such animal had actually been discovered by his son-in-law, he surely would have heard about it in Frémont's letters. But, since Frémont was by this time in California, the case was thrown out of court for lack of positive evidence—and the fuss that Senator Benton had kicked up drew even larger crowds of the curious to the show.

Finally, figuring that "Old Woolly" had earned retirement, Barnum put him out to pasture on his Connecticut farm—where he continued to be a source of amazement to everyone who passed.

Some time later, Barnum's neighbors were to see an even stranger creature toiling in Barnum's fields.

In 1849, P. T. conceived the idea of Barnum's Great Asiatic Caravan, Museum and Menagerie. In partnership with Sherwood Stratton, Tom Thumb's father, and Mr. Seth B. Howes, a well-known showman of the time, he dispatched an expedition to Ceylon for the purpose of bringing back a dozen or more elephants, "besides such other wild animals as they could secure."

At the end of a year, the ship returned to New York with ten fine Indian elephants, which Barnum paraded up Broadway in pairs, each team hitched to a chariot. Adding several animals and curiosities from the museum—including Tom Thumb, who went along as "patron"—the Asiatic Caravan traveled around the country, under canvas, for four years, returning handsome profits to Barnum's coffers.

When Barnum sold the show at the finish of its tour, he kept one elephant, which he sent to his farm in Bridgeport. There, in charge of a keeper dressed in Oriental clothes, it was set to the task of plowing Barnum's cornfields. The keeper was given a railroad schedule so that the elephant would always be hard at work whenever a passenger train passed by on the New York and New Haven.

As Barnum had intended it should, the story that "P. T. Barnum, proprietor of the celebrated American Museum in New York, has introduced elephants upon his farm to do his plowing and heavy draft work" made headlines in all the papers. Barnum didn't come right out and say so, but he allowed gullible reporters and visitors to believe that the pachyderm also cleared his fields, built his stone fences, and in fact did most of the heavy work on the place. In answer to thousands of letters from farmers all over the country, Barnum declared that elephants were the ideal work animal for American farms.

For some reason, the idea of elephants as farm animals failed to create a national agricultural revolution. But it paid off Barnum richly in oceans of free publicity for the museum.

In his years as the world's greatest showman, Barnum exhibited thousands of freaks—all the way from pinheaded Africans, to Wild Men from Borneo (who were really Hiram and Barney Davis, Negro brothers from Long Island); to families of "pure-white Africans, with white wool and pink eyes"; to Chinese women with bound feet; to Young Herman, the expansionist who could inflate his chest from thirty-eight to sixty inches. But the most famous freaks were the giants, the midgets, the Bearded Lady— and, most peculiar of all, the Siamese twins, Chang and Eng.

Ever since he opened the American Museum, Barnum had always had a giant or two on his stage. All of them, like his midgets, were well-formed and intelligent individuals, differing from normal people only in their size.

Barnum first heard about Ann Swan from a visitor to the museum who said that he was a native of Pictou, Nova Scotia, and that one of his neighbors had a seventeen-year-old girl who was nearly eight feet tall. Barnum sent an agent to Pictou to bring Ann back to New York. Her exact height was seven feet eleven inches and her weight was 413 pounds. She was just as pretty and intelligent as any ordinary girl of seventeen and her emotions were equally normal—which she proved a year or so afterwards by marrying a handsome young giant whom Barnum had christened Captain Bates.

Captain and Mrs. Bates remained in Barnum's employ for a number of years—long enough to save up a considerable nest egg—and after their retirement built a giant-sized house for themselves in a small town in Ohio.

General Tom Thumb had proved to be such a sensation from the day of his first appearance in 1843 that Barnum was constantly on the lookout for another midget who might be as talented and attractive. But it was not until eighteen years later, in 1861, that he found one precisely to his liking. And then it was the midget who found him, not he the midget.

A "sharp, intelligent, witty little fellow" called at the museum and asked to see the proprietor. He was ushered into Barnum's office, where he introduced himself as George Washington Morrison Nutt. He was eighteen years old, he said, and his father was Major Rodnia Nutt, a prosperous farmer in Manchester, New Hampshire.

Barnum whipped out a measuring tape and assured himself that the lad was just twenty-seven inches tall. Like Tom Thumb, he was perfectly proportioned.

Young Mr. Nutt informed the showman that several

offers had been made to him by other exhibitors, but that he would much prefer to work for the great Mr. Barnum. Barnum signed him to a three-year contract at $10,000 a year. The newspapers made much of P. T.'s new find, and referred to him as "the $30,000 Nutt."

Barnum conferred the title of Commodore upon him; and Commodore Nutt soon became almost as great a public favorite as Tom Thumb had been before him.

The world, unfortunately, is full of skeptics and non-believers. And before long the rumor began to make the rounds that there was no such person as Commodore Nutt —that Barnum was simply exhibiting Tom Thumb under a different name. History fails to clarify what part, if any, Barnum himself played in starting such tales. Barnum only tells us that when he tried to explain that these rumors were false, people simply did not believe him. The Commodore, from time to time, made certain "slips" that tended only to increase the doubts.

At last the time came, as Barnum put it, "to turn all doubts into hard cash by bringing the two dwarfs together and showing them on the same platform." For this purpose, Tom Thumb closed a Western engagement to appear at the museum for four weeks alongside the Commodore. As Barnum anticipated, the scoffers bought tickets as fast as the box-office clerk could hand them out.

But there was one thing Barnum hadn't anticipated. Over the years, the real Tom Thumb had added a few inches and several pounds, and many of the people who refused to be humbugged persisted in declaring that Commodore Nutt was indeed Tom Thumb, and that the genuine was an imposter. Much fun was had by all—and much money was made by P. T. Barnum.

Another of Barnum's show-business firsts was the original "bearded lady." But unlike many of the so-called bearded ladies that have been seen in circuses and sideshows from that day to this, Madame Josephine Clofullia was as feminine as any other woman, and not just a man in female dress.

Josephine had begun sprouting a beard when she was only a child. By the time Barnum hired her, at the age of twenty-five, her face was adorned with a long, luxuriant, curly set of moustaches and whiskers that would have made any Civil War general proud. She was married and the mother of a small son—who also had a fuzzy beard and whom Barnum displayed as the "dog-faced boy."

Audiences were amazed, but not unduly excited about her, until a paying customer, William Charr, sued Barnum for cheating him out of his admission fee, claiming that Madame Clofullia was not a woman at all, but simply a dressed-up man.

The trial was a public spectacle. Josephine's husband took the stand to swear that she was his lawful, wedded wife and the mother of his son. At Barnum's request, she was examined by a reputable New York doctor—in the presence of a New York City Police matron—who testified that she was in fact completely feminine. The case was dismissed, and Madame Clofullia became one of the museum's star attractions.

Even after a newspaperman revealed that "Humbug Barnum" had paid Charr to bring suit in the first place, the bearded lady continued to be a popular drawing card.

Barnum gave the language a new term when he coined the phrase "Siamese twins." Chang and Eng were certainly not the first pair of unfortunate babies whose bodies were joined together at birth. But they were the first that the world at large ever heard about—and so, even today, all such connected twins are referred to as "Siamese."

Born to poor Chinese parents at Bangesau, Siam, in 1811, the boys were attached to each other by a thick strip of muscle and cartilage located at the base of their rib cages. In spite of this handicap, they learned to walk, and even to swim, together. And it was while they were swimming in the river that ran by their village, that the skipper of a Yankee schooner spotted them one day. The captain, a man named Coffin, bought them from their aged mother with the idea of exhibiting them in Europe. The boys were then about nineteen.

In due time, after showing them for several years in England and on the Continent at modest profits, their owner brought them to New York, where Barnum first saw them. He gave Coffin a good price for their contract and arranged to exhibit them at the museum. The name under which they had always been billed, "The Siamese Double Boys," didn't strike P. T.'s ear quite right. He simplified it to "Siamese Twins"—and for many years thereafter Chang and Eng were museum favorites.

Although bound to one another for life, Chang and Eng were as unlike as any two humans could be. For the most part, Eng was the "good guy," Chang the "bad guy." Chang liked to drink, often getting himself riotously drunk, while Eng was a teetotaler. Yet even though they shared the same bloodstream and had only one liver between them, Eng never suffered any ill effects after one of Chang's bouts with the bottle. When one became ill, the other usually was perfectly all right. By nature, Eng was cheerful and easygoing, while Chang was inclined to be moody, nasty and irritable. They actually hated each other with a deep intensity that was to endure throughout their lifetime.

After Barnum began to make them wealthy, they lived for a single purpose: to find some way by which they could be separated. But doctors in America and Europe assured them that separation could result only in death for them both. They were finally forced to accept the fact that they would never be separated.

Shortly before the Civil War, with plenty of money in the bank, the twins quit the museum and bought a plantation near Mount Airy, North Carolina. There they lived as pleasantly as they could, and astounded the world by marrying Addie and Sally Yates, the daughters of a poor Irish sharecropper.

Now that they were family men, they built a second mansion on the plantation, so that one would be the home of Eng and Sally and the other the home of Addie and Chang. The twins divided their time equally between the two residences. As time went by, Chang and Eng became the fathers of twenty-one children, all physically normal.

When the War Between the States spread destruction over the South, the twins lost all their money and all the slaves who worked their acres. Although they had always detested the idea of being exhibited as freaks, they were forced to go back to Barnum and the museum. After a few years in New York and another profitable tour of Europe, they were able to retire again to the peace and quiet of Mount Airy.

By 1874, Chang's health had begun to fail rapidly, while Eng felt as fit and hearty as any normal man of sixty-three. Then one morning, when one of Eng's sons came into their room to awaken them, he discovered that his Uncle Chang had died in his sleep. Realizing that this meant his own death as well, Eng went into an uncontrollable fit of nerves. Before a doctor could be summoned to the plantation, he too was dead.

The Siamese twins were buried together, inseparable in death as they had been all through life.

Most of Barnum's exhibits were genuine freaks rather than fakes. But every now and then, as was the case of Colonel Frémont's Woolly Horse, P. T. liked to fool people just for fun—as well as for profit.

As the American Museum grew more popular, it was sometimes difficult to handle the huge crowds. The biggest problem was to get people to leave, once they had toured the exhibits, and thus make room for newcomers. This congestion was particularly annoying on weekends and holidays, when large families often brought their lunches, prepared to stay all day.

There appeared to be no solution until Barnum had another of his timely inspirations. Working at night, Barnum's carpenters cut an additional exit door through the far end of the lower hall into the street. Above this they hung a large sign which read: THIS WAY TO THE EGRESS! Rushing through the door to see what sort of weird oddity an "egress" might be, large portions of the crowd found themselves standing in Ann Street, outside the museum.

One of Barnum's most frivolous fakes was an exhibit which he himself publicly acknowledged was "a hoax of a hoax."

The original hoax was planned in 1868 by William Newell and George Hull, two patient confidence men. In that year they had a five-ton block of stone carved into the figure of a human giant. Using dyes and acid, they "aged" the carving and buried it on Newell's farm near Cardiff,

New York. The following year Newell began to dig a well over the burial site and "discovered" the stone giant. The newspaper publicity brought the curious and the "experts." Some scientists pronounced the Cardiff Giant, as it soon became known throughout the world, the petrified remains of an ancient man. Others declared the giant had been carved by prehistoric inhabitants of the area. And although reputable scientists denounced the giant as a hoax, Newell and Hull erected a tent over it and collected $1 per tourist.

Barnum offered $60,000 for the Cardiff Giant, but Newell refused. P. T. then engaged a sculptor to carve a duplicate, which he put on exhibit. When Newell sued Barnum for his hoax, Barnum's defense was that since the Cardiff Giant itself was a hoax, his was only a hoax of a hoax. Barnum won the case, and in spite of the public admission of his fakery, people continued to pay to see the fake fake.

No freaks at all, and only slightly fake, were the "Swiss" Bell Ringers. They were a group of musicians from Lancashire, England, whose only instruments were finely tuned bells of various sizes. When Barnum heard them on one of his many trips to London, he was fascinated by their unusual and delightful music, and signed them to a long-term contract.

Barnum decided that bell ringing didn't seem very English. Swiss, he thought, would appear to be more authentic. Therefore, he instructed them to grow long handlebar moustaches and wear Swiss mountaineer costumes. There was only one drawback, the musicians spoke English only. This didn't bother Barnum a bit, since the dialect used in Lancashire is quite unlike any English heard anywhere else in the world.

"Just speak in America as you are speaking to me now," Barnum told them, "and no one will recognize your speech as anything other than authentic Swiss."

Many teams of bell-playing musicians have appeared on the American stage since Barnum's time—and all of them, almost without exception, have been billed as "Swiss Bell Ringers."

Neither freak nor fake, but frighteningly real, were the Indian chiefs that Barnum exhibited in the museum for a short period in 1864. The chiefs, representing most of the Plains Indians tribes, had come east to Washington to talk peace terms with the Great White Father, Abraham Lincoln. Lincoln assured them—and he meant it—that certain lands in the Dakotas and Montana would always be their private domain, free forever from the encroachment of the white man.

The chiefs, pleased with the result of their meeting with the President, were delighted at Barnum's invitation to come to New York. Barnum, of course, had paid their interpreter a considerable sum in advance.

Although Barnum was very wary of them and a little nervous in their presence, he couldn't resist having some fun at their expense. In exhibiting them on his stage, P. T. would pat each of them in turn on the shoulder, tell the audience his name, and recite something of his past history.

Yellow Bear, in particular, was notoriously bloodthirsty. He and his warriors had massacred many a wagon train of white settlers on their way through the Plains to Oregon. When it came his turn to be introduced, Barnum would shake his hand, smile and pretend to be paying him the highest of compliments. But knowing that neither Yellow

Bear nor any of the others understood a word of English,
P. T.'s speech went something like this:

"This Indian, ladies and gentlemen, is Yellow Bear, chief
of the Kiowas. He has killed scores of white people and is
probably the meanest, most black-hearted rascal that lives
in the West. If the bloodthirsty little villain understood
what I was saying, he would kill me in a moment. But since
he thinks I am complimenting him, I can safely state the
truth to you that he is a lying, thieving, treacherous, mur-
derous monster. He has tortured to death poor, unprotected
women, murdered their husbands, and brained their help-
less little ones. And he would gladly do the same to you
or me if he thought he could escape punishment."

While the audience listened, horrified, Yellow Bear would
smile and bow, as if to say that every word Barnum spoke
was quite true.

One final note about Barnum's Indians. In the early
1870's, gold was discovered in Dakota and Montana, and
whites rushed in to the Indians' sacred ground in greedy
swarms. Unfortunately, these white intruders were backed
up by the United States Army, and the bloody Indian Wars
began.

Almost all of the chiefs who had sat on Barnum's stage
put on their war paint. And at least one of them, White
Bull, was with the Indian army that wiped out General
Custer's command at the battle of Little Big Horn.

Not all of Barnum's schemes for the greater glory of the
American Museum materialized.

Once he attempted a contest to find the most beautiful
girl in the United States—a forerunner of the modern Miss
America Pageant—but the project proved too involved and
difficult to manage.

While on a trip to England, he made a private deal to buy the house in which William Shakespeare had been born, intending to take it apart for shipping, then put it back together in New York and display it. But word leaked out and the British rose up in arms. It was purchased by the Shakespeare Association and kept as an English shrine.

On the same trip, he came within an inch of buying Madame Tussaud's famous wax museum and transferring the whole thing to New York. At the last moment, after papers had actually been signed, the enterprise fell through.

When the restoration of Pompeii was temporarily halted for lack of funds, Barnum offered to complete the excavation work at his own expense if he could exhibit any relics he found for a period of five years. The Italian government refused.

But none of these setbacks ever deterred P. T. in his constant quest for the rarest and most unusual things in the world.

What was Barnum's biggest attraction? Perhaps without knowing that he was doing so, he tells us about it in his autobiography.

"One one occasion," he relates, "I was sitting in the ticket office reading a newspaper. A man came in and purchased a ticket of admission. 'Is Mr. Barnum in the museum?' he asked. The ticket seller, pointing to me, said. 'This is Mr. Barnum.' Supposing the gentleman had business with me, I looked up from the paper. 'Is this Mr. Barnum?' he asked. 'It is,' I replied. He stared at me for a moment, and then, throwing down his ticket, exclaimed, 'It's all right! I have got my money's worth!' And away he went without going into the museum at all."

12

...e Art of Losing—and Making—Money

As long as P. T. Barnum stuck to show business almost everything he touched turned to gold. But when he strayed into some other kind of business, he seldom succeeded.

During the period after his adventures with Jenny Lind, P. T. played with a number of commercial enterprises.

One was a patented fire extinguisher, which succeeded only in burning down the building on which it was being tested. Another was a weekly newspaper, which lost money when he began losing interest in it. A third was a stock-holding venture in the New York World's Fair of 1853 which was a loser before it got started.

The money Barnum lost in these financial excursions was peanuts compared to the gigantic Jerome Clock swindle—the final splurge into big business that swept away his entire fortune.

In 1851, Barnum had dreamed a big dream. He decided to build a new city, every detail of which was to conform to his own personal blueprint. With William H. Noble as a partner, he bought 224 acres of choice land on a broad plateau directly across the Poquonock River from Bridgeport. The partners laid out the acreage in lots, crisscrossed it with tree-lined streets, and reserved several acres in the center for a public park. They called their new city East Bridgeport.

Every second lot was offered for sale at a bargain price—the same price, in fact, that the land had originally cost. The alternate, in-between lots the partners kept for themselves. Sales were made on condition that a suitable home, store or business building be erected within a year, and that it conform to a certain standard of architecture and landscape design approved by the sellers. Since Barnum had recently been converted to teetolalism, every buyer was also obliged to sign the pledge not to drink or smoke.

As an added inducement, Barnum and Noble advanced one-half, two-thirds, or sometimes all the construction money to people who were good credit risks. The partners thought their own profits would come from the sale of their reserved lots when property in the new city began to rise in value, as they were sure it would.

To Barnum's credit it must be emphasized that the East Bridgeport development was not altogether a quest for personal profit. He had a lot of money, all that he thought he would ever need for himself and his family. His new city, more than anything else, was intended as a public service. Obviously, the opportunity of adding to his balance in the bank ran a close second.

Barnum induced several manufacturing companies to

come to East Bridgeport, sometimes helping to finance them. As a result, more workmen flocked in and bought houses, and soon the little city began to grow.

Barnum admitted that he "had East Bridgeport on the brain. Whoever approached me with a project that looked to the advancement of my new city," he said, "touched my weak side and found me an eager listener."

It was in this euphoric spirit that he was touched by the tempting ticktock of Jerome clocks.

In the summer of 1855, Barnum decided to retire altogether from show business. Tom Thumb—remember that Barnum still owned 50 percent of his mighty midget—was a steady source of income. East Bridgeport was going ahead full steam. He was happy in his role of gentleman farmer at Iranistan.

Therefore he sold the American Museum collection and goodwill to John Greenwood, Jr., and Henry D. Butler. Sometime before, he had renewed his lease on the museum building for twenty-five years in his wife's name. As part of the agreement with Messrs. Butler and Greenwood, Charity would realize a continuing profit on it of $19,000 a year.

In the fall of the year of his retirement, Barnum was propositioned by Mr. Chauncey Jerome, president of the Jerome Clock Company. The company, it appeared, was thinking of moving its plant, along with about 1,000 workmen, to East Bridgeport. There was, however, a slight problem. Nothing serious, of course. Just a temporary inconvenience. The company needed $110,000 right away. If Mr. Barnum would be willing to sign a series of notes up to that amount, he certainly couldn't lose by it. Jerome Clock was as solid as the Rock of Gibraltar. And it would be a fine addition to the prosperity of P. T.'s new city.

Chauncey Jerome later declared that it could not have

been he who made the call, since he was retired at the time; it may have been his son, who succeeded him as president. But whether it was Jerome *père* or *fils*, Barnum was impressed. The company had a good reputation. Jerome clocks were sold all over the world. Chauncey Jerome had built a $40,000 church in New Haven with the idea of presenting it to the congregation. He was a rich man—or so it seemed.

Even so, at the outset, Barnum played it cagey. He asked to see the company's books and was shown an official report of the directors which showed that Jerome Clock had a capital of $400,000 and a surplus of $187,000—$587,000 altogether. It was explained that extra money was needed because the past year had been one of those rare bad ones, and the additional $110,000 would be used chiefly to avoid having to lay off employees.

It was understood that Barnum's maximum responsibility would be $110,000—and that, in the "impossible event" of his taking a loss, Chauncey Jerome would personally guarantee repayment. Then there was the big new factory and its 1,000 employees that would be added to East Bridgeport, and the comforting and humane thought that he, Barnum, could keep their jobs for all of them.

At the beginning, Barnum kept careful tabs on all the notes he signed. When the amount reached the stipulated $110,000, and he was called upon to sign several more notes, he refused to do so until he received in return an equal amount of his own previously signed notes that had been paid and canceled. The next day the canceled notes were brought to him, and he signed the new ones.

This procedure was repeated on several occasions—Barnum receiving canceled notes and signing new ones in their stead. He had a letter from the company secretary boasting joyfully that Jerome Clock would soon be in a position to "snap its fingers at the banks." A letter from the cashier of a New Haven bank expressed the highest confidence in the financial strength of the concern.

Barnum then began signing new notes without demanding to see the old ones. Too late, Barnum learned that he had been a victim of the oldest con game in the world— the quick-change shuffle. He had signed notes far in excess of every dollar he possessed.

With the collapse of Barnum's paper bridge, the Jerome Clock Company collapsed too. Even after absorbing Barnum's fortune, it finally paid off at only about 12 cents on the dollar. In one of the many editions of his autobiography, written years afterwards, when Barnum had made an even bigger fortune and was once again on top of the world, he wrote, rather naively:

"And to cap the climax, it never removed to East Bridgeport at all, notwithstanding this was the only condition which ever prompted me to advance one dollar to the rotten concern."

It is pleasant to find that all friends are not fair-weather ones. Although from time to time Barnum saw people ducking quickly into doorways to avoid him as he walked along New York streets, his really loyal friends offered him loans to get him back on his feet again. Others wanted to stage benefits for him. Tom Thumb, on tour, offered to drop everything and return to New York to do anything he could. But Barnum said a grateful "No, thank you" to all these overtures. He was determined to pull himself back to solid ground by his own bootstraps.

All of his property, including Iranistan, the mortgages he held on the museum, and his share in New Bridgeport, was assigned to creditors to be sold at auction. The only loan that Barnum accepted was used to repurchase property in his new city from the assignees. In the end he managed to buy it all back—and New Bridgeport, in turn, repaid him royally, eventually bringing him more money than he had lost in the entire Jerome Clock fiasco.

Meanwhile, using some of Charity's money, Barnum rented a small house in New York. He was constantly in the courts, hauled up by speculators who had bought some of his notes at discount in the mistaken belief that Barnum must surely own some hidden assets and that they could be paid face value without going through the slow and uncertain process of waiting for the sale of his property. To all of this, Barnum submitted with patience and as much good grace as he could muster.

One lawyer who had represented several of Barnum's persecutors especially got under his skin.

"What is your name, sir?" he asked with a supercilious air for about the two-dozenth time.

"Phineas T. Barnum."

"What is your business?"

"Attending bar."

The little lawyer's brows went up at this answer. "And where do you attend bar, and for whom?"

"I attend the bar of this court nearly every day," Barnum replied, "for the benefit of two-penny, would-be lawyers and their greedy clients."

In an effort to raise some money with which to pay off his debts, Barnum left his slow-moving affairs at home in the hands of trusted friends and took Tom Thumb on another tour of Europe. The General, after his long absence, played to crowded houses in England, France, Germany and Holland—and Barnum was able to send home sizeable sums to pay off his obligations.

Then, when he was back in New York, misfortune again struck a shattering blow.

Iranistan had remained closed and unoccupied for almost two years. James D. Johnson, a friend of Barnum's and one of his assignees, wrote to say that since there seemed to be little probability of selling the house in the near future, the Barnum family might as well move back in until a sale was made.

Barnum agreed, and engaged a group of painters and carpenters to get the house in order. Because of the presence of so much paint and linseed oil all over the place, the workmen had strict orders not to smoke on the job. But at about midnight on December 17, 1857, Barnum's beloved Oriental villa burst into flames and by morning was nothing but a heap of ashes.

Iranistan had cost Barnum a minimum of $150,000. Because he had allowed some policies to lapse, at the time of the fire there was only $28,000 of insurance coverage. This, along with $50,000 which Elias Howe, the inventor of the sewing machine, paid for the grounds, went to the clock note-holders.

Once more, P. T. went back to England, where he had left Tom Thumb in charge of an agent. But since Tom and the agent were doing a turn-away business in towns all through England, Scotland and Wales, Barnum soon found himself with time on his hands. He began to look around for another novelty he could sell.

He found it quite by accident, and almost as a joke.

One evening he was sitting around an exclusive London

club with several friends, drinking tea as they sipped their after-dinner brandy.

One of them suggested that Barnum get up a lecture on some subject such as, say, the Art of Money-Getting.

Barnum roared. "You've got it all wrong! Considering what I've been through the last couple of years, I'd do better with the Art of Money-Losing."

He was reminded, however, that no one can lose money without first making it; and that nothing interests the average man as much as the trick of making a fortune.

Later, alone in his room, the clocks began to tick in his head. He needed the money, that was for certain. So why not give it a whirl? He picked up a pen and a piece of hotel stationery and began working up a rough draft.

The first lecture on the Art of Money-Getting was delivered at St. James' Hall in Piccadilly. Barnum had advertised it lavishly, and when he walked out on the stage to the podium, he noticed with a satisfied eye that the huge hall, which could hold 3,000 people, was completely filled. In the front rows he saw many of his old friends, including William Makepiece Thackeray, who had come to wish him well.

The lecture was half serious and half fun, and spiced throughout by dozens of anecdotes about his early life and his show-business career. At the end he was roundly applauded. And the next day all the London papers gave him enthusiastic notices.

After several more appearances at St. James', P. T. gave lectures through the provinces, always to large and enthusiastic crowds. It appeared that P. T. Barnum was as big a drawing card as any of his attractions had ever been. "The lecture itself," he commented, "was an admirable illustration of the Art of Money-Getting."

Early in 1860, after five grueling years, Barnum had paid off every cent of his Jerome Clock debts. Now he was ready to start all over, and he was determined to stick with the business he knew inside and out, the business that he had almost single-handedly invented: show business.

Greenwood and Butler had not done well with the museum. They had bought Barnum's show, but they couldn't buy his know-how and his flair. When Barnum proposed that he buy them out, they agreed to his terms.

Overnight, blazing posters and screaming headlines proclaimed:

Barnum is on His Feet Again!

The New York public impatiently fingered the quarters that were burning holes in their pockets. They couldn't wait to see what "Old Humbug Barnum" had in store for them this time around.

13
Grizzly Bears and White Whales

AND so we see Phineas Taylor Barnum—fifty years old now, inclining a bit to portliness, nose a little more bulbous, balding head fringed by curly gray hair, no longer the boy wonder but with blue eyes still twinkling with youthful enthusiasm—ready to take on the world again, and raring to go.

The newspapers, as always, were on his side. The Boston *Gazette* burst into flowery doggeral in its lead editorial, as follows:

> *Barnum, your hand! The struggle o'er,*
> *You face the world and ask no favor;*
> *You stand where you have stood before,*
> *The old salt hasn't lost its savor!*

And so on until the poet ran out of journalistic iambic tetrameter.

He opened the American Museum with the usual Barnumian blare of advertising trumpets. It was announced that on opening night Mr. Barnum himself would personally present a mysterious novelty never before seen on any stage. When P. T. made his appearance the museum was filled to standing-room capacity.

In the center of the stage, on a small table lay a large canvas sack that obviously contained a squirming live animal. Barnum stated that one of his assistants had purchased a rare, "cherry-colored" cat from a farmer, that he himself hadn't yet seen this unusual creature, but now he was going to "let the cat out of the bag" so that everyone could see it together. He loosened the string and out popped an ordinary coal-black alley cat.

Barnum pretended to be outraged at such a hoax. Then the assistant stepped forward and explained, so all could hear, that the up-state farmer had meant no hoax at all. That the cat was the exact color of *black* cherries.

As the audience held its sides and howled with laughter, Barnum put it to a voice vote. Should he pay the farmer and keep the cat, or throw it back into the nearest alley? He got a unanimous "Pay the farmer!"—and the cat, wearing a fancy collar inscribed "The Cherry-Colored Cat," became a permanent exhibit.

After this bit of tomfoolery, Barnum introduced his feature attraction—the first of a series of stage plays that were eventually to make the greatly enlarged Lecture Room of the museum New York's most popular theater. The plays that Barnum presented during the ensuing years were of a kind he called "moral drama." He prided himself upon the fact that none of them contained vulgarity or profanity.

Among his biggest hits were *Uncle Tom's Cabin, Moses in Egypt, Joseph and His Brethren,* and *The Drunkard.*

Later, Barnum presented a few of Shakespeare's plays, but only after he personally had seen to it that any "objectionable or questionable" scenes and lines were stricken out or rewritten. Barney Williams, Mary Gannon, and the great Shakespearean actor Edward Sothern, all won their fame and popularity on Barnum's stage.

One of the favorite all-time Barnum presentations was "Grizzly Adams and His Trained Grizzly Bears."

James C. Adams was an authentic frontier "character." He had started out as a hunter and trapper in the Rockies and the High Sierras. There he had single-handedly captured and trained more than two dozen grizzlies, along with a few California black bears, wolves, buffaloes and elk. The grizzlies, especially one named "General Frémont," were mean and treacherous even after Adams had taught them to go through their bag of tricks. And Adams had paid dearly for their training. He had been mauled, torn and battered by the beasts. Upon first meeting Barnum, he took off his wolfskin cap. An entire segment of the top of his skull had been bashed away, and underneath its thin protective layer of membrane, the showman could see Adams' brain working and pulsating.

"That looks like a fatal wound, Mr. Adams," Barnum said in amazement.

"Yep!" Adams replied. "It was nearly healed, but old Frémont opened it up again for me just before we left California. I don't reckon I've got more'n about six months or a year left. I'm purt' nigh used up."

Grizzly Adams and P. T. became equal partners in the show—Grizzly handling the animals, and Barnum handling all managerial arrangements.

Instead of exhibiting the act in the museum, Barnum decided to show it under canvas in a vacant lot on a Broadway corner. On the morning of the opening, a brass band led the parade of Adams' animals up Broadway to the showgrounds. Grizzly, dressed in a brand-new buckskin hunting costume adorned with fringe and animal tails, rode fearlessly on General Frémont's back. Thousands lined the street to watch the procession—forerunner of the grand circus parades that were later to be such a spectacular part of the Greatest Show on Earth. And thousands paid the admission price to go inside and see old Grizzly whip and beat his dangerous animals into obedience.

During the first six weeks of the showing on Broadway, Adams grew weaker with every day that passed. His wife, who had been living in Massachusetts, came to New York to nurse him. Barnum's own doctor attended him daily, dressed his horrendous head wound, and vainly advised him to quit before he dropped dead. But the old man's spirit refused to be quenched, although he was in constant pain and ran a fever which progressively got higher.

Grizzly Adams hung on to the tattered shreds of his life for another three months with the tenacity of a bear hug. Then, laughing and kidding Barnum to his last pain-ridden hour, assuring him that "I'm going to live a dang sight longer than the doctors think for," the old mountain man collapsed and died.

Barnum bought his grizzlies and other animals for the museum, thus assuring a degree of security for the old frontiersman's widow.

One day Barnum read in the *Sun* that some fishermen up in the estuary of the St. Lawrence River had captured a live white whale. P. T. had recently read Herman Melville's *Moby Dick,* and the idea of exhibiting a living, spouting, white whale in the museum fired his imagination. Monsieur Guillaudeu, his resident scientist, informed him that it was quite possible to keep such a whale alive for the five-day journey by freight car from Isle aux Coudres, Quebec, to New York in a tank of saltwater and seaweed—provided that an attendant stood by with a bucket and a sponge to keep the sea beast's mouth and blowhole constantly wet.

Barnum determined to capture not one, but two, white whales—a male and a female. He ordered that a brick-and-cement tank, forty feet long and eighteen feet wide, be built in the museum's basement to house the monsters once he got them to Broadway and Ann. Although he knew nothing about capturing whales, and even less about their care and feeding, the thought of failure never entered his mind.

When he arrived at the island with two assistants, he found it inhabited by friendly and curious French-Canadian fishermen-farmers who spoke not a word of English. However, when he walked down to the water's edge he was delighted to see the spouting of dozens of whales as they played only a few hundred feet offshore where the salty tides of the Atlantic mixed with the fresh outflow of the St. Lawrence.

Using a combination of his meager French and of sign language, Barnum managed to hire a dozen or so fishermen to trap his whales for him. He agreed to pay them a daily wage, plus a liberal bonus if they were successful.

Barnum's plan was to lay out a V-shaped trap in a shallow place, with the wide end pointed toward the water and the narrow end toward the shore. The idea was to let the whales swim into the open end, then, once they were inside, to close it by having his men row out in boats and make such a splashing with their oars that the whales would be afraid to attempt to swim back out the way they had come. Once the tide receded, the creatures would be trapped almost high and dry and could be secured by slipping a running noose over their tails and towing them to the shipping tanks.

"All this looked simple enough on paper," Barnum recalled. But executing the plan was a different, and quite frustrating, matter. For several days Barnum and his crew stood by prayerfully as scores of whales swam around the trap as though trying to sniff out what it was all about. On several occasions, a few ventured inside, but retreated before the fishermen could man their boats.

Then early one morning several days later, Barnum was awakened by a great chorus of gibberish-French triumph. Two beautiful specimens were inside the trap, and the tide was ebbing so that they were unable to get out. Carefully following Barnum's instructions, the men managed to transfer the whales to the shipping tanks and put them aboard a sloop which would take them to the nearest railroad on the mainland.

Leaving his aides to escort the precious cargo to New York, Barnum paid the promised bonuses and left for Quebec City. There he wired dispatches to the New York newspapers about the "first daring capture of living white whales," and had copies delivered to the local paper. He did the same in Montreal. In addition, he alerted each town and village along the route as to exactly what time on what day the "whale train" would pass through. Every station along the way was mobbed by curious crowds who "came to the cars to see the whales that were traveling by land to Barnum's Museum in New York. Those who did not see the monsters with their own eyes, at least saw someone who had seen them. And I thus secured a tremendous advertisement, seven hundred miles long, for the American Museum."

Upon his arrival in New York, Barnum put up a bulletin board at the entrance of the museum to which he tacked the dispatches that came hourly from the whaling expedition. Copies also went to the papers. When the whales at last were swimming freely in the basement tank, such crowds as Barnum had never seen came pouring into the museum.

Unhappily, they were living in fresh water and stagnant air, and not even Professor Guillaudeu knew what or how to feed them, so the poor creatures died within a week. Undiscouraged, Barnum decided to try again.

At a cost of several thousand dollars—plus another thousand to certain city aldermen—Barnum laid a system of iron pipe under the city streets from the museum to the ocean waters of New York Bay. He then built a special whale tank on the museum's second floor. This was made of heavy slate slabs, and had viewing windows of inch-thick French glass. After its completion, a second pair of whales arrived from Quebec. The saltwater of the bay, pumped in by Barnum's pipes, suited them much better. And when they too died—"Their sudden and immense popularity was too much for them," Barnum announced—they were replaced from the endless supply that disported themselves off the shores of Isle aux Coudres.

The live whales were sensational, and immensely profitable. But—leave it to Barnum!—skeptical letters began appearing in the press declaring that the beasts were not whales at all, but in reality only extra-large porpoises. When these reports had circulated to P. T.'s satisfaction, he asked Professor Louis Agassiz, the world-famous curator of the Museum of Comparative Zoology at Harvard University, to come down to the museum for an official appraisal. The professor gave Barnum a certificate declaring that his exhibits were genuine white whales, which was at once included in all museum advertising.

Meanwhile, Barnum imported "the first and only genuine hippopotamus ever seen in America," and displayed him in the basement tank. The hippo was advertised as THE GREAT BEHEMOTH OF THE SCRIPTURES—causing thousands of ministers, Bible students, and other "cultivated people" to join the daily lineup at the museum's ticket window.

Now, with a constant supply of seawater at hand, Barnum began to add sharks, tortoises, sea horses and rare tropical fish to his marine collection. In addition, he bought out Boston's Aquarial Gardens and brought its specimens to the museum.

In less than a year, P. T. Barnum was back, spending money as if it grew on trees, and raking it in faster than he was able to spend it.

The first few years of Barnum's spectacular comeback, the years of his greatest success with the museum, also happened to be the bloodiest years in American history. To millions the Civil War brought tragedy, privation, and death. But to Barnum it brought only prosperity. This was purely coincidental, for Barnum was a staunch Union man —and, for all his humbugging, an honest man—and would have had no part of any plan to turn the circumstances of the conflict to his own advantage. But the war made New York City more affluent than it had ever been before, and put more money into the pockets of New Yorkers with which to buy such luxuries as entertainment.

Although the City of New York sent many distinguished regiments into battle, many New Yorkers wanted no part in the struggle. Mayor Fernando Wood, a violently anti-Lincoln Democrat, fought to have the city secede from both New York State and the Union and declare itself a Free City empowered to trade impartially with both sides.

The powerful antiwar feeling in New York had its climax in the draft riots of midsummer 1863. Mobs of rioters roamed the streets, setting fire to the homes and business establishments of prominent Union supporters and hanging innocent free Negroes to lampposts amid shouts of:

"String up the niggers!"

"They caused the war!"

Barnum himself was an active member of the pro-Union "Prudential Committee," and during the troubles often had military guards assigned to protect his home. But the draft rioters did not attempt to damage the museum. A year later, however, he was not so lucky.

Late in 1864, the Confederate government made a desperate, last-ditch effort to carry the war to the North. The attacks were launched from C. S. A. military headquarters in Toronto, Canada. A daring daylight raid was made by Southern cavalry officers, dressed in civilian clothes, on the sleepy little village of St. Albans, Vermont. The raiders robbed St. Albans banks of more than $2,000,000 and escaped back across the Canadian line. A number of United States steamships were sunk in Lakes Ontario and Erie. But the biggest project of all was the attempted burning of New York City in retaliation for General William T. Sherman's incendiary march through Georgia to the sea.

The Confederate raiders had counted on the help of the several thousand New York members of the Sons of Liberty, organization of Southern sympathizers better know to history as the Copperheads, whose emblem was the head of the Goddess of Liberty cut from a copper one-cent piece and worn as a badge of mutual recognition. At the last moment the plot was betrayed by a turncoat Confederate. A division of Union troops was marched into the city and the scheduled Copperhead uprising was squelched before it got started. However, half a dozen Southern officers who were in New York to head up the Copperheads' activities decided to go it alone.

Armed with 1864 versions of the Molotov Cocktail—glass bottles filled with highly inflammable liquid—the raiders planted fire bombs in dozens of hotels, theaters, business buildings and docks. Barnum's museum, though not on the original list of targets, got it by accident.

Because the fire bombs did not work as well as expected, city fire companies managed to get the conflagrations under control. Meanwhile, excited crowds began milling around in confusion all up and down Broadway—and one of the arsonists found himself caught in a crowd at the entrance to the museum. He bought a ticket and tried to lose himself among the customers inside.

Once in among the exhibits, it occurred to him that Barnum's famous museum would make a prime and effective target. Taking a glass bomb out of his carpetbag, he hurled it against the nearest wall. Flames and thick, black smoke immediately threw the customers into a panic, and the bomber made his escape in the confusion. Later identified as Captain Robert Kennedy, C. S. A., he was captured by Secret Service men, tried for espionage and arson, found guilty by a military court, and hanged.

Since firemen got to the source of the flames without too much delay, Barnum's loss was light. He estimated it at only about $1,000. But this fire was just a prelude to the disaster that was to befall the museum less than a year later.

In 1865, Barnum was elected to the Connecticut State

Legislature, where he became a dedicated enemy of what he believed to be a less-than-honest railroad monopoly. While making an impassioned speech on July 13, 1865, a page handed him a telegram. It stated that the American Museum was in flames and that its total destruction was certain. He read the message, put it in his pocket, finished his speech, waited until his bill had been voted upon and carried, and then rushed to the depot and caught the first train to New York. The museum was a smoldering heap of ashes.

The fire, started by a wayward spark in the basement engine room, had quickly surged upward to envelop the entire building. Samuel Hurd, the assistant manager, rescued the cashbox containing several thousand dollars. The customers and all the human freaks were led out the exits in good order by city firemen. Anna Swan, the giantess, was lowered from the third floor by means of a derrick. The firemen released hundreds of exotic birds, including parrots, condors, vultures and eagles, who flew in panic over the unfamiliar city rooftops. Many of the menagerie animals suffocated in the billowing clouds of smoke or were burned to death in their cages. A tiger leaped from an upper-floor window and was brained by a fireman's axe. A dozen or so rattlers, and other snakes both poisonous and harmless, wriggled frantically up Broadway and scattered the gaping crowds that were watching.

Barnum later wrote: "It was a sad sight indeed. Here were destroyed, almost in a breath, the accumulated results of many years of incessant toil, my own and my predecessors', in gathering from every quarter of the globe myriads of curious productions of nature and art—an assemblage of rarities which a half million of dollars could not restore, and a quarter of a century could not collect. In addition to these there were many Revolutionary relics and other links in our national history which never could be duplicated. Not a thousand dollars' worth of the entire property was saved; the destruction was complete; the loss was irreparable. My insurance was but $40,000, while the collection, at the lowest estimate, was worth $400,000. When the fire occurred, my summer dramatic season had just begun and the museum was doing an immensely profitable business. My first impulse, after reckoning up my losses, was to retire from active life and from all business occupation beyond what my large real estate interests in Bridgeport would compel."

In an editorial in his New York *Tribune,* Horace Greeley wrote: "There are still fishes in the seas and beasts in the forests; birds still fly in the air and strange creatures still roam in the deserts; giants and pygmies still wander up and down the earth; the oldest man, the fattest woman, the smallest baby are still living. And Barnum will again find them."

And Greeley was right. Barnum couldn't quit a second time. For one thing, he had 150 employees who would be thrown out of work. For another, he truly believed, deep down, that New York City needed, and deserved, a really first-class museum—and that only he could provide it.

Within weeks, he had leased three buildings on Broadway and started converting them into an even larger museum than the old one. He sent agents all over the world looking for new rarities, oddities and curiosities. He bought up several entire museums. He still had his living freaks, and his successful company of actors and actresses.

Barnum's New American Museum opened its doors at sunrise on November 13, 1865. Maybe the 13th was unlucky. Maybe he should have waited one more day.

For two and a half years Barnum's New American Museum grew and prospered. Barnum added new attractions as fast as his operatives could round them up. He engineered a merger with the renowned Van Amburgh Menagerie Company which, years later, would become the nucleus of the "Greatest Show on Earth." But for the most part the museum was so successful—and Barnum's aides and associates had been so thoroughly schooled by him—that things pretty well ran themselves without the old master's constant personal attention. This left him plenty of time to pursue what had become his favorite occupation: the lecture circuit.

He spoke on "Success in Life." He dusted off the old "Art of Money-Getting" with which he had always had so much fun. But his favorite topic was "Temperance." Having taken the pledge many years before, Barnum's fight against liquor and drunkenness became a crusade.

In one Iowa town, a little old lady came backstage after he had spoken and confessed that she and her family had traveled some thirty miles in a carriage to hear him.

"Are you sure, madam," Barnum asked with a grin, "that you came to *hear* me rather than to *see* me?"

"Well, to tell you the truth, Mr. Barnum," she confessed, "we have all read so much about you, and your museum, and your queer carryings-on, that we were not quite sure but what you had cloven feet and horns on your head. But, la, me! I don't see but what you look a good deal like other folks after all."

On the bitter cold morning of March 3, 1868, as New York City cuddled under a heavy blanket of new-fallen snow, Barnum sat with his wife at the breakfast table glancing through the paper. A headline caught his eye.

He blinked a couple of times in amazement, then remarked quietly:

"Hal-lo! Barnum's museum has burned."

Charity smiled. "Yes. I suspect it had."

"It's a fact." Then he read the headline aloud: "BAR-NUM'S MUSEUM TOTALLY DESTROYED BY FIRE."

P. T. showed so little outward excitement at this momentous news that his wife assumed he was joking. She remarked:

"Yes. It was totally destroyed two years ago, but Barnum built another one."

"Quite true. And now *that* one has burned. Just listen to this." And he proceeded to read the whole story.

Incredible as it seemed, the new museum had been burned to the ground, a total ruin, during the night. Barnum was shocked, but not as much as the first fire had shocked him. Despite the severe financial loss, Barnum said that his first reaction was regret for the poor animals of the menagerie that had burned to death in their cages.

Like the other one, this second fire had begun in the building's basement, and the fury of the flames was so intense, their progress so rapid, that the entire contents of the museum were destroyed before firemen could get at the blaze. The few people on the premises at that late hour had been lucky to escape with their lives.

Even when the firemen got to the scene with their equipment, fighting the blaze was useless. The cold was so intense that water from the fire hoses froze as soon as it struck the building's walls. The front granite wall, the only part of the museum left standing, along with the lampposts on the Broadway sidewalk "were covered in a gorgeous framework of transparent ice, which made it altogether one of the most picturesque scenes imaginable. By moonlight the ice-coated ruins were still more sublime."

The above quote is Barnum's own description. Indeed, a man must possess the soul of a poet to see such beauty in the wreckage of his property.

Once again Barnum thought seriously about permanent retirement. The three fires, Iranistan and the two museums represented a total loss of about one million dollars. The money of course was no consideration. Barnum's second fortune had been much larger than his first. But the destruction of both his magnificent museums dampened his spirits. A number of men offered to shoulder the financial load if only he would create and manage a third museum. He took Charity for a long vacation in northern New England to think things out in the clear, crisp mountain air. Then an old friend, George Wood, offered him a tempting middle-of-the-road way out of his dilemma.

George Wood was a successful manager who had already begun remodeling a large building at the corner of Broadway and Thirteenth Street in which to house a museum and theater. He offered P. T. a thumping salary, plus a bonus based on gate receipts, simply to give him the benefit of his experience and act as his general adviser. The only string that Wood attached was Barnum's promise to have no active interest in any other museum in New York.

It was perfectly obvious that Wood's chief objective was to have Barnum shelved as an active competitor. This was fine with P. T., and he jumped at the offer. Now he could retire gracefully and become a gentleman of leisure, and at the same time allow the fingers of his left hand to dabble in show business.

Yes, now he'd take things easy. No more hustling to put new shows together. No more financial headaches. No more *anything*—except riding around East Bridgeport in his carriage admiring the new city he had created, entertaining old friends in the evenings, delivering an occasional lecture when the mood struck him, sitting by the fire with a good book on wintry mornings while other less fortunate men struggled through snowdrifts to put in long days at their offices.

Yes, from now on Phineas Taylor Barnum was going to live the life of Riley!

14

The Sawdust Trail

AFTER being evicted from Iranistan in 1855 by the Jerome Clock creditors, P. T. and his family lived in a suc-
cession of boardinghouses and small rented dwellings. Then,
five years later, his fortune rebuilt, he constructed a rela-
tively modest home not far from the site of his old Oriental
villa. He called it Lindencroft.

About the time of his "retirement" Charity's health declined rapidly, and the doctor declared that she would feel
better if she lived nearer to the shore. Barnum sold Lindencroft and built a lavishly ornamented mansion near Bridgeport's Seaside Park—a resort area for local people which
he himself had been instrumental in creating. This home
he christened Waldemere, or Woods-by-the-Sea.

East Bridgeport was booming, growing in value every
day and vastly enriching Barnum as it grew. Invested capi-

tal, Barnum always claimed, was like an orchard full of fruit trees. It worked twenty-four hours a day for its owner whether he kept a close eye on it or not. A number of large factories had been built in the new city, and thousands of workmen had invested in building lots and homes.

At Waldemere, Barnum hosted large weekend parties. He entertained friends at dinner. He attended operas and concerts in New York. He dropped by the Wood Museum now and again, but he found that he wasn't essential, or even much needed, in the conduct of its affairs. Finally, he admitted to himself that he was being bored stiff.

He took a party of friends on a leisurely trip through the West, where he stopped off to lecture at Council Bluffs, Omaha, and Salt Lake City. While in Salt Lake, he was invited to the palatial home of Brigham Young, the Mormon leader. At that time, polygamy was an accepted doctrine of the Mormon Church, and Young was reputed to have twenty-seven wives and scores of children.

Governor Young was in a jovial mood when he received P. T.

"Barnum," he asked jokingly, "what will you give to exhibit me in New York and eastern cities?"

"Well," Barnum replied, "I'll give you half the receipts, which I guarantee will be $200,000 a year. I consider you the best show in America."

In Kansas, Barnum organized a buffalo hunt under the auspices of George Armstrong Custer, the boy-general of the Civil War, who was then in command of Fort Hayes. It would be eight years before Custer would keep his fatal appointment on a slope above the Little Big Horn River.

Custer outfitted Barnum and his party with guns and horses, and assigned a company of cavalry as their escort.

The buffalo hunt offered Barnum a "sensation," as did the rest of the western junket. "But sensations," he lamented, "cannot be made to order every day." And boredom between sporadic sensations was not for P. T. Barnum. His pent-up energies were at the boiling point.

During the fall and winter of 1870-1871, P. T. got together Barnum's Great Museum, Menagerie, Caravan, Hippodrome and Circus, which he opened under canvas on a three-acre lot in Brooklyn on April 10. Following a spectacularly successful opening, he took it on the road for the rest of the summer in states from Maine to Kansas. Five hundred horses and men were needed to transport it over the country roads. In November, he brought it back to the Empire Rink in New York, where it played to capacity houses until after the holidays.

That winter Barnum worked with all his old verve and vitality to double the circus' size. From Europe he brought in shiploads of animals and variety acts. From Alaska came giant sea lions and "barking seals," which "weighed a thousand pounds each and consumed from sixty to a hundred pounds of fish daily." The creature of his sideshow was "The Four Wild Fiji Cannibals, ransomed at great cost from the hands of a royal enemy by whom they were about to be killed and perhaps eaten."

The circus was now much too large and cumbersome to be transported by horses and wagons. So Barnum came up with another "first." He made arrangements to have the entire show—tents, seats, animals, performers, roustabouts and managerial staff—travel by rail. It took sixty to seventy freight cars, six passenger cars and three engines to get the show on the road. But the advantages were well worth the expense of transportation. On rails, the show could travel as much as 100 miles a night, and thus reach a good-sized town every day. Each morning, while the tents were being readied, the circus paraded through the town's main streets, drawing thousands of townspeople out to the grounds to see one of the three daily performances. Since the arrival of the circus was publicized weeks in advance—by huge, glaring posters on country barns, street banners, window displays and floods of printer's ink in the local papers—customers drove in by horse and buggy from as far as 100 miles around.

At the end of the outdoor season, Barnum brought the circus back to New York to a gigantic showplace on Fourteenth Street which he had leased, called the Hippotheatron.

There, after a gala and successful opening, his old nemesis, fire, struck Barnum a heavy blow for the fourth time. Starting once more in the basement boiler room of the building in the middle of the night, the flames destroyed everything except two elephants and a camel.

Barnum was at breakfast when he got the bad news. He called immediately for cablegram blanks and wired his European agents to send him replacements for all of the animals that had been lost. In addition, he authorized them to spend up to an additional $500,000 to secure specimens that had never before been seen on this side of the Atlantic, as well as any and all rarities and curiosities that they could come up with.

Then he finished his breakfast.

In April, 1873, only three months after the fire, Barnum hit the sawdust trail again with an even bigger circus than he had fielded the year before. It was so huge that expenses were more than $5,000 a day. From all sides, friends predicted that such a staggering overhead would surely bankrupt him. Barnum's reply was simple and it reaffirmed the basic credo of his show-business faith.

"I suppose," he said, "that there is a limit beyond which it would be fatal to go in catering to the public's instruction and amusement, but I have never yet found that limit."

The 1873 season proved that he was right. His tents covered double the amount of ground that they had occupied before, and they were always packed to capacity. In September, at the end of the tour, Barnum decided to return to Europe—not only to have a brief vacation, but also to see what additional attractions he could uncover on the Continent.

While in Germany, Barnum received a cable from his son-in-law announcing that Charity, his wife of forty-four years, had died on November 19. Although Charity had long suffered from ill health, Barnum was shattered. He cabled instructions that her coffin be placed temporarily in a vault in the Mountain Grove Cemetery, in Bridgeport, there to await his return from Europe for the final burial services.

Home once more, Barnum tried to console himself with hard work. While he was in Europe, his managers had informed him that a lease could be had on a piece of land in the center of New York—the entire block between Madison and Fourth avenues, and Twenty-sixth and Twenty-seventh streets—and that the kind of building which he had in mind, the world's largest indoor arena, could be erected for about $200,000. Barnum cabled an immediate okay, and so his Great Roman Hippodrome staged its premier performance in mid-April.

The show was as lavish as Barnum had visualized it. It opened with a grand procession which Barnum called the

Congress of Nations, a representation of the pomp and circumstance that surrounded most of the kings, queens and potentates of history. All were costumed with historical accuracy, and were followed by armies and retinues that comprised more than 1,000 men and women and perhaps twice that number of animals. Dozens of bands blared forth appropriate musical accompaniment.

The opening was followed by horse races, chariot races, steeplechases, performing elephants, wild-animal acts, acrobats, wire-walkers, trapeze artists—all in all a show that, in Barnum's less-than-modest judgment, "will probably not be witnessed again in this generation."

Barnum was wrong. He himself was later to put on shows that topped it.

The Hippodrome could seat 10,000 people, and it was always sold out days or weeks in advance. President and Mrs. U. S. Grant came up from Washington to see the spectacle, along with the entire Cabinet.

After a prolonged engagement in New York, Barnum took the show on the road—under canvas and by rail, as before—and brought it back to New York to play the winter months.

In November, 1874, only a year after Charity's death, Barnum married again—this time an English girl who was forty years his junior. She was Nancy Fish, the lovely daughter of P. T.'s old friend John Fish of England, a millionaire textile manufacturer. He had first met Nancy when she was only eight years old.

After years of living with the near-invalided Charity, whom he had loved deeply and devotedly, Barnum found Nancy was like a tonic. She liked riding and boating. She enjoyed driving with him in his carriage, and he delighted in showing her off to his old friends. She was a gracious and vivacious hostess at Waldemere and in Barnum's New York town house. Unlike Charity, who had never gone with him on his many whirlwind tours, Nancy liked to travel the circus trail, and she loved the thrill of circus life as much as he did.

She went with him on all his trips through the United States and abroad. Nancy gave him back his youth—and she remained faithful and devoted throughout the seventeen happy years of their marriage. After his death she completed the last few chapters of his autobiography, an unfinished task that had worried him during his final illness.

For six years after he opened the Great Roman Hippodrome, Barnum's circus was his life—interrupted at intervals by short vacations with Nancy, occasional lecture engagements, and interludes of politics.

He was elected Mayor of Bridgeport in 1875 and served one term, after which he declined to run again. He was twice more elected to the Connecticut General Assembly. He donated a massive brick-and-stone museum to the city of Bridgeport—which still stands today and is filled with many of the curiosities that he had collected throughout his years as a showman.

Whenever foreign nobility came to the United States, one of the first sights they wanted to see was Barnum's Great Roman Hippodrome and Traveling Circus. One such guest was David Kalakaua, King of the Sandwich Islands, now the State of Hawaii.

Barnum sat with the King during the performance, at which about 12,000 people were present. Halfway through the show, apparently recognizing the royal visitor, the audience rose to its feet and began shouting, "The King! The King!" then, "Barnum! Barnum!"

At this, Barnum ordered an ornate carriage driven up to the entrance to his box. He and the King stepped into it and circled the arena to the roars of a tremendous ovation. The King was pleased. "In all of us," he whispered as he bowed and waved to the cheering crowd, "there is somewhere an actor."

Barnum added to the show with every new idea that flashed through his racing brain. He exhibited the first "Human Cannonball," an English girl named Rose Richter who, as Mademoiselle Zazel, was shot out of a wooden cannon into the air and was caught by her partner as he hung by his knees from a trapeze.

He introduced "Captain Costentenus, a Greek nobleman, who was tattooed from head to foot over every inch of his body in Chinese Tartary, as punishment for engaging in rebellion against the King." The Captain had suffered punishment all right—for the complete job had been done by New York tattoo artists in about two months.

An aeronaut named Professor Donaldson thrilled the crowds with daily balloon ascensions from the circus lot. One day in Chicago, he took along an enterprising reporter from the *Journal* as a passenger, disappeared into the clouds over Lake Michigan, and was never seen or heard of again.

Every morning, before the start of the parade, a salute of thirteen guns was fired from a private battery of cannon—just in case anybody had forgotten that Barnum was coming to town. Each night the performance concluded with a spectacular fireworks display.

Until 1880, Barnum had no circus competition worthy

of the name. His Great Hippodrome, Traveling Circus and Menagerie overshadowed every other show on the road. Some of them he bought. Others failed for lack of business. A few struggled along the back-country roads managing to eke out an existence.

Then one day P. T. met an opponent who, he said, was "worthy of my steel." He was a bright young man with enormous energy, business talent and ingrained showmanship. His name was James A. Bailey.

Out of this confrontation the immortal partnership of Barnum and Bailey was born. And it had its beginnings in an argument about a baby elephant.

15

The Greatest Show on Earth

I N a land of small horse-and-wagon circuses, Barnum had been undisputed king. But in 1880 a new traveling show, almost as big as Barnum's, invaded the American scene. It was known as the Allied Shows, and was a merger of The Great London Circus, Sanger's Royal British Menagerie, and Grand International Allied Shows. Its owners were three young men named James E. Cooper, James L. Hutchinson and James A. Bailey.

Allied Shows had created an international stir when they took their circus on a two-year world tour, showing with immense success in South America and Australia, before touring America's largest cities. In their New York engagement they stole a march on the Old Master by illuminating their show with electric and calcium lights instead of old-fashioned gas lamps.

Barnum paid them the grudging compliment of saying that "they had adopted my manner of dealing with the public, and consequently their show grew in popularity."

It was Bailey who was the promotional and directorial genius of Allied. Small in stature, prematurely balding, shy and retiring, he was a complete contrast to the big, jolly Barnum. He was an efficiency expert. Barnum was the Great Showman.

Bailey was born James A. McGinnis. Legend has it that, when they first became partners, Barnum insisted that McGinnis change his name to Bailey so that the dual name of the circus, Barnum and Bailey, would be alliterative and eye-catching. But the fact is that when McGinnis' father died, the boy was befriended by a small-time circus man named Frederick Bailey and subsequently took his name.

The two men first met when one of the Allied elephants, Hebe, became the mother of the first baby elephant ever born in captivity. The public became excited over the baby elephant, and Allied's box office take rose sky-high.

Usually in circumstances like this Barnum bought his rival off. But when he wired "the lucky proprietors," as he called them, an offer of $100,000 for mother pachyderm and her child, Bailey wired back a sassy refusal in which he suggested, in effect, that Barnum go jump in the nearest lake. To add insult to injury, Bailey enlarged P.T.'s telegram and displayed it in big posters and advertisements with the headline:

What Barnum Thinks of the Baby Elephant!

Barnum, so long a one-man world as far as the American circus circuit was concerned, recognized a real threat. Since it didn't appear that he could buy 'em, the only thing left was to join 'em. He arranged a meeting with Cooper, Hutchinson and Bailey.

The meeting was cordial, friendly and unusually brief. Barnum declared that he was delighted to find men who were comparatively young and who possessed business talent and energy approximating his own. After a few days of ironing out details, the deal was consummated. At first the name for the combined shows was The Barnum and London Circus. Then, after an interval, Cooper and Hutchinson sold out for enough money to make them reasonably independent—and the circus became THE BARNUM AND BAILEY GREATEST SHOW ON EARTH.

The new show opened in the original Madison Square Garden on Monday, March 18, 1881. The buildup for the grand opening was a spectacular parade up Broadway on the Saturday before. No procession like it had ever been seen. The whole gorgeous panoply of The Greatest Show on Earth was on public view—animals by the thousands, gaily decorated circus wagons, clowns, beautiful girls, acrobats, Indians, brass bands, a calliope—all illuminated by calcium and electric lights. Half a million people jammed the sidewalks and windows along the route.

More than 100 newspaper editors and feature writers were brought by Barnum to New York, all expenses paid, to view the parade and the opening performance at the Garden. The dispatches they sent back to their papers were so filled with superlatives that readers all over the country couldn't wait for The Greatest Show on Earth to come to their towns.

After a successful engagement indoors in New York, the circus took to the road. It was necessary to enlarge the big tent area three times to handle the crowds. Railroads along the route ran special excursion trains from outlying towns—

often fifty miles distant—to the cities in which the circus was showing. And despite the added tent facilities, thousands had to be turned away at every performance.

"Frequently," Barnum recalled, "public and private schools, as well as factories, were closed on 'Barnum Day,' school committees and teachers recognizing that children would learn more about natural history by one visit to our menagerie than they could acquire by months of reading."

Nothing like The Greatest Show on Earth had ever been seen before in the world. And it was only a foretaste of the flamboyant success which the Barnum and Bailey Circus would enjoy over the remaining ten years of Barnum's life.

In Washington, President James A. Garfield came to see the show. He watched the fabulous circus with boyish enthusiasm and delight. And when he saw a huge poster that bore Barnum's picture and a caption that said beneath it: THE CHILDREN'S FRIEND, he exclaimed: "Yes! Mr. Barnum is the Kris Kringle of America!"

The Greatest Show on Earth closed its 1881 season in Newport, Arkansas, in November, and went into winter quarters at Bridgeport.

During the winter, Quene, the matriarch of Barnum's twenty-two elephants, gave birth to a tiny son, who thus became the second elephant ever born outside its native habitat. The little fellow weighed only 145 pounds at birth, and Barnum named him Bridgeport in honor of his birthplace. When the 1882 season opened, Bridgeport was the star of the show.

Of all the aspects of circus life, elephants were Barnum's favorite. And it was with an elephant that P. T. Barnum reached the height of his circus career. That elephant was the immortal Jumbo, without doubt the most famous elephant in all animal history.

Jumbo had been captured when he was little more than a calf in the bush country of East Africa and sold to a professional animal dealer. The dealer sold him to a Paris zoo, which in turn traded him to the London Zoological Society in return for a rhinoceros. At the time he went to London, Jumbo was an inconspicuous four feet in height.

Jumbo lived in the London Zoo for seventeen years, during which time he grew to prodigious size. In 1882, he weighed seven tons, stood twelve feet high at the shoulders, had a trunk seven feet long—and when he reared his tremendous head and extended his trunk, he could nibble leaves from a tree branch that was twenty-six feet above the ground he stood on. No elephant of his size had ever been seen, in captivity or out.

His appetite was as enormous as his bulk. Each day he ate 200 pounds of hay, several bushels of oats and other grain, more than a dozen loaves of bread—along with sundry tidbits such as vegetables, fruits and all the peanuts that admiring visitors to the zoo would give him. He washed this down with countless buckets of water and a daily quart of whiskey.

Jumbo was a favorite with London's children. They rode in a huge basketwork carriage on his back, while his trainer perched on his large head and guided him by tickling him behind the ears with an elephant hook.

Once Barnum had taken a ride on his back, but the idea that the London Zoo would part with its most popular resident did not enter his head at that time. Later one of Barnum's agents approached the superintendent of the zoo and asked if Jumbo could be bought. "Mr. Barnum," said the agent, "will pay a good, round price for him." But the superintendent simply scoffed at the suggestion.

Then, for the first and only time in his life, Jumbo went into a period known as "must," a condition that sometimes causes male elephants to become irritable—and frequently dangerous—during the mating season. The Zoo superintendent feared that Jumbo could conceivably go raging mad and become what is known as a "rogue." In that case, he would have to be destroyed. This caused him to reconsider selling Jumbo to Barnum. He suggested a price of $10,000.

The agent cabled Barnum and received the reply: "I will give ten thousand for Jumbo, but the Zoo will never sell." P. T. was nearly bowled over when he learned by return cable that his offer had been accepted. That same day he had his London bankers give the Zoo authorities a check in that amount. Jumbo was his!

The English people rose up in arms against such an unheard-of piece of sacrilege. A snowstorm of indignant letters from schoolchildren and adults engulfed the Zoo authorities. Editorials denouncing Barnum, from the great *Times* of London to the smallest country weeklies, flowed forth. The London *Standard* likened Barnum to a Southern Simon Legree who would break up slave families by selling Negro children and parents to different buyers at the auction block. Writers mourned the fact that the beloved Jumbo would be removed from his gentle world of quiet strolls over the soft grass on the Zoological Gardens and condemned to a lifetime of drudgery as a Barnum freak.

Queen Victoria and her eldest son, the Prince of Wales, both of whom were old friends of Barnum, urged that the contract for Jumbo's sale be broken and promised that any damage fees Barnum might demand would be gladly paid by the British public. Schoolchildren started to save up their pennies to buy Jumbo back. The question of Jumbo was even raised in England's House of Commons.

The editor of the London *Daily Telegraph* cabled Barnum to name his own price for canceling the sale. P. T. cabled a reply as follows:

> To LeSerge, *Daily Telegraph,* London.
>
> My compliments to the editor of the *Daily Telegraph* and the British nation. Fifty-one millions of American citizens anxiously awaiting Jumbo's arrival. My forty years invariable practice of exhibiting the best that money can buy makes Jumbo's presence here imperative. One hundred thousand pounds would be no inducement to cancel the purchase.
>
> P. T. Barnum

Editor LeSerge reprinted the cable in the *Telegraph,* along with the sad comment that "Jumbo's fate appears to be sealed." Crowds flocked to the Zoo to see Jumbo for the last time—with the result that the total of the modest admission fees to the Zoo was increased by an incredible $2,000 a day.

A Fellow of the London Zoological Society—a contributing member or stockholder—brought legal action in the British Chancery Court to prevent Jumbo's sale. But after a court hearing, the sale was pronounced valid.

"All England," Barnum said, "seemed to go Jumbo-mad. Pictures of Jumbo, the life story of Jumbo, a pamphlet entitled 'Jumbo and Barnum' and all sorts of Jumbo stories and poems, Jumbo hats, Jumbo collars, Jumbo neckties, Jumbo cigars, and Jumbo fans were sold by the tens of thousands in the stores and streets of London and other British cities. Meanwhile, London correspondents of the leading American papers cabled column upon column on the subject, describing in complete detail the sentimental Jumbo craze which had seized upon Great Britain."

All of this, in turn, created a reaction on this side of the Atlantic. America's leading newspapers urged Barnum to keep Jumbo at all costs. Thousands of letters from people all over the country, mostly from children, begged Barnum for the opportunity of seeing Jumbo for themselves.

"The only burning question at this time between England and America," said the Honorable James Russell Lowell, United States Ambassador to the Court of St. James, "is Jumbo."

At last the day came when Jumbo was to say farewell to his London home. Like all captive elephants, Jumbo was extremely timid and nervous. When Barnum's trainers led him out through the gates of the familiar Zoological Gardens, he began to trumpet wildly and tried to reenter the Zoo. When he discovered that the gate was closed, he lay down in the street and refused to be budged.

Barnum's agent cabled the boss in New York: "Jumbo has lain down in the street and won't get up. What shall we do?" Barnum cabled back: "Let him lie there for a week if he wants to. It's the best advertisement in the world."

After twenty-four hours of confused whimpering that sounded almost like a child crying, the gates were reopened and Jumbo was allowed to return to his quarters. Now the trainers began to figure out a way to move him by strategy.

They constructed a gigantic ironbound cage with a door at each end and mounted it on wheels designed to hold up an enormous weight. With the doors open, the cage was backed up to Jumbo's den, and its wheels sunk into the ground so that the floor of the cage was level with the floor of the elephant's quarters. Thus Jumbo had to go through the cage to get outdoors. For some days he looked at the narrow passageway with suspicion. Then, at last, he followed his keeper through the cage to take his daily airing. This procedure was continued for several days until Jumbo's fears were stilled.

Then one day, when he was inside the passage, the doors of the cage were closed. Now the wheels were dug free of the ground and Jumbo was slowly hauled away to the steamship, where an entire deck had been remodeled to make room for him.

Calmed with whiskey and beer, Jumbo took the rough Atlantic voyage well, arriving in New York safely and in good spirits on Sunday morning, April 9. During the first two weeks at Madison Square Garden he created such a sensation that box-office sales, over and above the normal daily receipts, more than made up for the $30,000 which it had cost Barnum to buy him and transport him from zoo to circus.

The popular magazine *London Fun* took England's defeat with traditional British sportsmanship and good humor. It printed a redesigned royal coat of arms on which Jumbo replaced the British lion, and the motto of England was changed from *Dieu et Mon Droit* (which means God and my Right) to *Dieu et Mon Jumbo.*

Below the drawing was this paragraph:

"On account of the national interest manifested in Jumbo, we presume the British Lion is for the time being forgotten; and we therefore suggest the above as the most appropriate coat-of-arms for England."

16

The Death of Jumbo

JUMBO was the biggest attraction ever presented by The Greatest Show on Earth. From the financial point of view, he was a seven-ton gold mine. In his first season, in New York and on the road, he brought $1,750,000 to Barnum and Bailey's box office. And his popularity grew even greater during the remaining three years of his life.

Every morning he led a parade with an American flag grasped in his trunk. He waved it back and forth and up and down, and the children squealed with delight. Youngsters lined up to take turns riding atop his broad back. And carrying them, he seemed to be having as much fun as they were. Never did he become unruly or dangerous, as the London Zoo superintendent feared that he might. He was just a big, fat, happy-go-lucky beast.

And he contributed the adjective "jumbo" to the American vocabulary.

Jumbo also helped the circus roustabouts load and unload the tons of equipment from the flatcars that carried the show. With his enormous strength, he could push a loaded wagon as easily as a modern tractor.

His special pal was a small dwarf elephant called Tom Thumb. Barnum started out exhibiting the two together to emphasize Jumbo's huge dimensions. The big elephant and the little one became fast friends, and Tom Thumb tagged around after Jumbo whenever he could. They traveled together from town to town in a railroad car built especially for them.

On September 15, 1885, the show was ending its season in the town of St. Thomas, Ontario, and the cars were being packed for the trip back to Bridgeport and winter quarters. As Matthew Scott, the chief elephant handler, was leading Jumbo and Tom Thumb along a railway spur to their private car, the engine of a special freight train roared down upon them out of the darkness. The engineer slammed on the brakes, but it was too late. Scott managed to leap to one side of the tracks. Jumbo tried to butt his little friend out of the way, and as he did so, the engine struck him head on. His skull was fractured and his tremendous body smashed. Thanks to Jumbo's quick action, Tom Thumb sustained only a broken leg.

The loss of his star attraction was a blow to Barnum. That evening he wired Professor Henry A. Ward, the distinguished head of Ward's Natural Science Establishment in Rochester, New York. Professor Ward was the leading authority on the then infant art of taxidermy. The next day Ward sent his best taxidermist to St. Thomas to see what he could do about preserving Jumbo's body for posterity.

The professor's most promising assistant was a young fellow named Carl Akeley. In later years, Akeley was to become world-renowned as the "father of modern taxidermy," one of America's foremost big-game hunters, and the founding genius of Akeley Hall in New York City's American Museum of Natural History. But on this brisk September morning when he met Barnum in St. Thomas, he was just a gangling youth, beginning to put into practice the theories that were later to transform the awkward business of stuffing animal skins into the fine art that taxidermy has become today.

"I know this is a tall order," Barnum said. "But if you can do it, I want Jumbo mounted on a platform that can be wheeled through the streets at the head of the parade. And he has to look like he's *alive,* not just stuffed elephant skin."

First, Carl Akeley hired half a dozen professional butchers from local meat markets to remove the skin and extract the bones. At every step, he made careful measurements and accurate sketches of each part of the elephant's anatomy. After the fat and flesh had been meticulously scraped away from its underside, the skin was put into vats of curing solution and shipped, along with the bones, to Rochester. (When Jumbo's remains were buried, his stomach was found to contain hundreds of English coins.)

At Ward's, the skin was worked down to a uniform thickness of half an inch for easy handling. Then it was given a final curing treatment.

Meanwhile, working from his sketches and measurements, Akeley constructed a skeleton of sturdy oak beams. Over this, he built up an outer structure of thin wooden strips, steamed so that the wood could be shaped into the exact contours of Jumbo's body. The skin, now soft and and easily worked, was nailed to the wooden body in such a manner that the nailheads were concealed by the lifelike wrinkles and folds.

The job required five months of hard and painstaking work. But when it was done, Barnum and Akeley had brought Jumbo back to "life."

Jumbo may still be seen today—although somewhat the worse-for-wear—in the Natural History Museum of Tufts College in Medford, Massachusetts. His skeleton is in Akeley Hall in New York's American Museum of Natural History.

After Jumbo was killed, Barnum began looking around for another super-elephant that might replace him. Then he remembered Alice, who had been Jumbo's "wife" in the London Zoo for many years. (When Jumbo was removed from the Zoo in his cage, Alice had set up such a groaning and trumpeting of grief that her raucous caterwauling had excited and frightened all the other wild animals within earshot.)

Barnum bought Alice and brought her to the States, where he exhibited her alongside the mounted effigy of Jumbo and billed her as "Jumbo's widow." Alice didn't seem to recognize the revived Jumbo as her erstwhile mate, but the pair became one of the most interesting attractions of the 1886 circus tour.

For a long time, P. T. had been trying to buy a sacred white elephant of Siam. These beasts, regarded as holy, demigodlike creatures by the Siamese people, were naturally very difficult to obtain. The first white elephant that Barnum's agents were able to get was poisoned by the priests who attended it rather than have it fall into the hands of "infidels."

On his second try, Barnum had better luck.

In Mandalay, he bought a sacred elephant, called Toung Taloung, and had it shipped out of the country under the royal warrant of Burma's King Thebaw. Along with it he brought an orchestra of Burmese musicians to play their tinkling, unharmonious brand of music, and a band of Buddhist priests dressed in ceremonial costumes. He also obtained an official document, signed by the King's Master of Elephants which authenticated the royal character of the animal.

Until Toung Taloung's arrival, Barnum, like all Americans, had assumed that sacred Siamese white elephants were pure white—and he had made much of this unique coloration in his advance advertising and full-color picture posters. But much to his dismay, he discovered upon its arrival that the so-called white elephant of Siam is not actually white at all. Instead, it is a sort of dirty gray, with spots of light pink here and there on its body, and the pink eyes of a rabbit.

To the reporters who had accompanied him to the dock, Barnum could only say half-heartedly: "Well, it's whiter than I thought it would be." Then he added, in true Barnum style, "God made that white elephant, boys. But I assure you that if he had been made by Mr. Bailey or myself, he would be as white as the driven snow."

In 1885, General U. S. Grant, ex-President of the United States, was in desperate financial trouble. After leaving the White House, he had been misled into lending his name to a bogus Wall Street venture. When it collapsed, Grant was bankrupt. In order to extricate himself he had to turn over all his assets to satisfy his creditors, and these included the ceremonial swords, trophies and other valuable mementos that had been presented to him by grateful Americans and

by the people and rulers of dozens of countries he had visited during a trip around the world.

Hearing that these trophies would soon be out of Grant's
hands, Barnum at once wrote the General a letter and
dispatched it by special messenger. In it, he offered to
exhibit these treasures "in an elegant and suitable manner
throughout the civilized world." He added that "while you
would confer a great and enduring favor on your fellow
men and women by permitting them to see these trophies,
you could also remove existing embarrassment in a most
satisfactory and honorable manner." Barnum offered an
advance payment of $100,000 in cash, a generous share
of the profits, and a bond of $500,000 for their safekeeping
and return.

When P. T. called at Grant's home for his answer, the
General informed him that the trophies had already been
pledged and were no longer under his control.

After the conversation had turned to more pleasant matters, Barnum remarked:

"General, since your journey around the world you are
the best known man on the globe."

"No, sir," the General answered. "Your name is familiar
to multitudes who never heard of me. Wherever I went,
among the most distant nations, the fact that I was an
American led to constant inquiries whether I knew Barnum."

Barnum liked to be at the circus performances as often
as he could. He especially enjoyed seeing the children,
who almost invariably recognized him.

"To me," he wrote, "there is no picture so beautiful
as ten thousand happy, smiling, bright-eyed children; no
music so sweet as their clear ringing laughter."

He also liked to sit unnoticed in the audience, especially when the show was on the road, where he could hear the comments of the country folks who were seated all around him. One afternoon he was sitting in the bleachers directly behind an old farmer and his wife. As Barnum later told the story, their conversation went something like this:

"I declare, Sally," the man said. "I ain't seen a circus since I was twenty-one. And I never thought I'd see such wonderful things as I've seen today."

"I never seen a circus since I was a little gal," Sally replied. "But I was determined to see Barnum's. It certainly does beat all!"

The farmer reflected for a moment. "One thing I'd like to see is Barnum himself."

"Well, maybe you will. They say he sometimes goes on with his show."

Just about then, a young rider came into the ring standing on top of four spirited show horses and put on a dazzling exhibition of equestrian acrobatics.

At the conclusion of the act, the farmer swung his hat in the air, turned to his wife and exclaimed excitedly: "I'll bet five dollars that's Barnum! There ain't another man in America who could do that but Barnum himself!"

It is said that some individuals are "accident-prone," that somehow or another, whatever they do, accidents just naturally follow them around. If there is any truth in such a supposition, then P. T. Barnum was "fire prone." About ten o'clock on the night of November 20, 1887, the fourth fire of his show business career all but wiped out The Greatest Show on Earth at its winter quarters in Bridgeport.

How the conflagration started remains a mystery. Before the firemen arrived the huge building was reduced to a heap of ashes. Thirty of Barnum's thirty-four elephants managed to escape, as did two lions. One of them, Nimrod, went quietly out with his keeper. The second escaped by himself to the safety of a neighboring farmer's barn. There he attacked a cow and a calf. Aroused by the noise, the farmer grabbed his shotgun and killed the beast as he was enjoying a meal of fresh beef and veal.

Alice, Jumbo's "widow," was one of the four elephants that failed to make it. Toung Taloung, the sacred white elephant, got out but at once rushed, terror-stricken, back into the flaming building. He was driven out two or three more times, but each time he ran back in, and was last seen standing just inside the big door, thrashing his trunk and trumpeting in agony until a section of the roof collapsed on top of him. An elephant cow, Gracie, raced to the icy waters of Long Island Sound, where she swam around in circles until morning. Finally towed to shore, she died in a few hours.

Aside from Nimrod and the thirty surviving elephants, the entire menagerie was gone.

A few days after the fire, Barnum went into Bailey's office and found his partner leafing through a pile of telegrams and cables, and frantically writing notes.

"What are you doing that's in such a hurry?" Barnum wanted to know.

Bailey handed over a fistful of wires. "These are from animal dealers all over the world, telling us what they have available and what they can get us on short notice. So I'm ordering a new menagerie."

"And you're doing it all in one day?"

"Certainly," Bailey assured him. "By opening day next spring we'll have a bigger and better circus than we've had before."

And that's exactly what Barnum and Bailey did.

17

The Curtain Falls

Barnum was now getting old. He was a millionaire many times over, and he had earned a rest. But his mind hadn't lost its pep and vigor—and he couldn't resign himself to a life of loafing.

In the winter of 1889, when he was nearly eighty years old, he allowed himself one last show-business spree. He and Bailey packed up The Greatest Show on Earth—at a cost of more than a quarter of a million dollars—and took it to the huge Olympia arena in London.

Barnum feared that the English might still remember Jumbo, and perhaps even blame him for the animal's death while on the circus trail. But he needn't have worried. The engagement was a smash hit from opening day until closing—the most tremendous success of his long and lucrative career in the world of entertainment.

All his old friends came to see the show, and to see him personally. Queen Victoria, now entering her seventies, came to sit in the royal box, along with the grown-up Prince of Wales. Dukes, earls and lesser nobility of all ranks attended in droves. The Olympia could seat 15,000 spectators, and it was crowded at every performance.

Midway in each show, Barnum would appear and ride around the arena in an open carriage, smiling and waving to the people. At his appearance, the show would momentarily come to a halt, and the acrobats and trapeze artists and all the other performers in the three rings would stop what they were doing and join the audience in a standing, ear-splitting ovation. Then, as Barnum exited, the show would go on again.

London was his final fling. From then on he stayed pretty close to home—entertaining as often as he could get old friends together, taking leisurely trips with Nancy, dropping in on the circus now and then to see the show and count the house.

But for the most part he worked at bringing his autobiography up to date. The last paragraph of its latest edition, published in 1888, had begun with these words: "As I close this volume I am more thankful than words can express that my health is preserved, and that I am blessed with a vigor and buoyancy of spirits vouchsafed but to few; but I am by no means insensible to the fact that I have reached the evening of my life. . . ."

But Barnum didn't really believe that the evening shadows were closing in upon him. He would not admit, even to himself, the possibility of his own death. He believed that he still had a long way to go—and that he owed it to the public to keep them up to date on everything that he was doing.

He continued to get daily floods of mail, from fans all over the world as well as from personal friends. He was especially proud of one letter that had been simply addressed:

Mr. Barnum,
America.

It had been mailed in Bombay, India, and was dispatched halfway around the world to Waldemere in Bridgeport.

Midway in November, 1890, upon his return from a short vacation at his ranch in the West, he collapsed and was put to bed. The doctors said it was an acute attack of congestion of the brain.

But P. T.'s recuperative powers were remarkable. In a week or so he was able to be up and around for a few hours every day, reading the New York papers, writing, sending new ideas for the circus to Bailey in New York. It was too cold for the usual daily drives in his carriage, but he spent long minutes at the windows of his room, looking out over the big estate, and beyond its grounds to the sparkling gray waters of the Sound.

The winter of 1890 dragged on into the spring of 1891. The first green buds began to appear on the maple trees outside his windows, and the early daffodils poked up their yellow heads from the tidy flower gardens. But now Barnum spent most of his time in bed. He could feel his strength ebbing swiftly away. And although he never mentioned it, even to Nancy, he now knew that he was dying.

One afternoon he said to a visitor: "You know, the papers always go out of their way to find nice things to say about people in their obituaries. I'd like to see what they'll write about me after I have gone."

The friend reported this conversation to the editor of the *Sun,* who promptly wrote Barnum asking his permission to print his obit in advance "so that you can enjoy reading it."

The idea tickled Barnum. It was just the kind of shenanigan that he might have come up with himself.

On March 24, Barnum read his copy of the *Sun* with unabashed delight. Prominent on the front page was a headline:

GREAT AND ONLY BARNUM
He Wanted To Read His Obituary
Here It Is

Below was a long, detailed story of the highlights of Barnum's life, from his early boyhood, through his museum days, to his Greatest Show on Earth.

On the morning of April 7, Phineas Taylor Barnum lay under silken comforters on his large, high-posted bed of hand-carved cherry wood. One of his three doctors sat silently in a corner of the room. Nancy was in a chair beside him, gently patting his big, bony hand from time to time. The window curtains were drawn, letting in only thin slivers of the early spring sunshine. Barnum's eyes were closed. His breathing was faint. Now and then the ghost of a smile played about his lips.

Perhaps he was remembering his first big dream, which had been shattered in the boggy mire of his fabled Ivy Island. Maybe he remembered Coley Bertram that morning in the little New York store, telling him about the old slave that had been little George Washington's nurse.

Or perhaps it was Charity, and that wild ride home to Bethel through the lightning-splintered night.

Surely he thought of Nancy, for he opened his eyes just briefly, squeezed her hand and whispered: "My last thoughts are of you."

But they weren't. His last thoughts were where his heart had always been. Just before the final breath came from his worn-out body, just an instant before his great heart beat for the last time, he said in a voice so low that it was barely audible:

"Ask Bailey what the box office was at the Garden last night."

And then the final curtain fell on the greatest showman of them all.

Barnum was dead. They carried his casket to Mountain Grove and laid him beside Charity. The procession to the cemetery was a quiet one, for he had had enough of pomp and parades.

Yes—Barnum, the man, was gone. But he lives on in legend, and in the priceless legacy he left behind him.

He broke the taboo that said ordinary people shouldn't have fun and enjoy themselves. He bequeathed Hollywood and Broadway and the Big Top to the generations that would come after him.

And the legend of Barnum will keep on living as long as circus bands play and acrobats fly through the air and happy-faced children spend their dimes for peanuts to feed to the elephants.

Index

The Author

FELIX SUTTON grew up on a farm in West Virginia and was graduated from the West Virginia University School of Journalism. He has been a sportswriter, general reporter, and advertising copywriter. For the past decade he has devoted his talents to full-time free-lance writing. Mr. Sutton, who has written more than forty books and numerous magazine articles, now lives in New York City.